Everyman, I will go with thee,
and be thy guide

THE EVERYMAN
LIBRARY

*The Everyman Library was founded by J. M. Dent
in 1906. He chose the name Everyman because he wanted
to make available the best books ever written in every
field to the greatest number of people at the cheapest possible
price. He began with Boswell's 'Life of Johnson';
his one-thousandth title was Aristotle's 'Metaphysics',
by which time sales exceeded forty million.*

*Today Everyman paperbacks remain true to
J. M. Dent's aims and high standards, with a wide range
of titles at affordable prices in editions which address
the needs of today's readers. Each new text is reset to give
a clear, elegant page and to incorporate the latest thinking
and scholarship. Each book carries the pilgrim logo,
the character in 'Everyman', a medieval morality play,
a proud link between Everyman
past and present.*

MORE POETRY PLEASE!

100 POPULAR POEMS
FROM THE BBC RADIO 4 PROGRAMME

Foreword by
P. J. KAVANAGH

Compiled by
MARGARET BRADLEY

EVERY
J. M. DEN
By arran
British Br

First published in Great Britain, 1988
Reprinted 1991
Reissued 1993
Reprinted 1994 (three times), 1995, 1996, 1997

© Introduction P. J. Kavanagh, 1988

© Selection J. M. Dent and the BBC, 1988

Printed in Great Britain by
The Guernsey Press Co. Ltd
Guernsey
Channel Islands
for
J. M. Dent
Orion Publishing Group
Orion House
5 Upper St Martin's Lane, London WC2H 9EA

British Library Cataloguing-in-Publication Data
is available upon request.

ʌN
ᵗ • LONDON
gement with the
ɔadcasting Corporation

CONTENTS

INTRODUCTION

by P.J. Kavanagh

In the best and most interesting sense this book, with its predecessor, *Poetry Please!*, makes up the most democratic selection of verse ever put together. The poems in other anthologies are chosen by editors; here it is the public that has done the choosing, by asking to hear these poems read on the 'Poetry Please!' radio programme.

It is not necessarily the 'poetry-reading' public that writes in. This is sadly small anyway. A surprising number of requests come from people who make it clear they have read little or no poetry since they left school. But they remember a poem, or perhaps several poems (sometimes they remember them word for word), that was read to them years ago by a favourite teacher, and ever since then they have longed to hear it read again. Although this suggests they were somehow given the impression that poetry belongs to the world of childhood, and not to the real world of work, these listeners of long ago, who have been able to love and remember a poem all their lives, are the ideal readers of poetry, for whom every poet longs.

Another value of this collection is that it brings together not only rarities (the poem with which it begins is new to me) but universal favourites that are widely scattered and sometimes troublesome to find. Here, among others, is 'Kubla Khan', 'I remember, I remember', 'My Last Duchess', 'The Journey of the Magi', 'The Hound of Heaven'. Here are writers as diverse as Gerard Manley Hopkins, Louis MacNeice, George Herbert and Noël Coward.

Not every poem here is as good as its neighbours. Of course not; this is a democratic selection and all the better for it. There is sentimentality sometimes, and jokiness, and tumpity-tump tales. As for these last, how cheerful it is to come upon the schoolboy in Alfred Noyes's 'The Old Grey Squirrel', who 'lived in a cottage by the sea

> And the very first thing he could remember
> Was the rigging of the schooners by the quay.'

That is not the sort of poetry-noise you hear often nowadays.

The one unifying factor of these poems is that somebody (sometimes many people) loved one of them enough to remember it and want to hear it again.

It is interesting to see proved here what we like best in poetry, new and old. We like a strong feeling, a story and a strong rhythm. We also like sublety and surprise. But above all, almost without exception in these poems, we like a solid shape, a sense of musical structure; for that, after all, is what makes a poem stick in the mind.

This book is for the general reader, but it could also be of great service to schoolteachers who cast about for poems that might appeal to their pupils. These have proved their appeal, to non-scholarly people, and among them are some of the finest poems in the language.

MORE POETRY PLEASE!

Anon
From AGAINST WOMEN

Woman is by aptitude
destined to servitude;
extremely cruel and proud
she's by no reason bowed
by law nor governance cowed;
of her dowry boastful
of each good way neglectful
of idle paths she's heedful.

She'll do nothing in its day
observes no middle way;
she lies down if she's stroked
and leaps up if provoked;
a white hot flame in ferment
like ice in disappointment,
she'll do no wanted thing,
she's storm without ending.

Woman is full of devil's prattle
and her tongue of empty tattle;
and her distaff as a rattle
she'd beat Arthur in a battle.
Lewd she is and prodigal,
fickle, vain and cruel,
clattering complaints perpetual,
yet she grants what isn't legal.

Full of disdain and violence,
ostentation, arrogance,
envy and covetance,
caprice and instability;
she's eager to do injury,
revels in lies and luxury
and takes revenge extempore.

She'll elevate Eve's throne
higher than Snowdon's crown;
she'll boast the thing she knows not
and what she knows she shows not.

If you'll but attend
to the tales I append
you will understand
that there's no deed unplanned
by a woman's hand.

Helen caused the stitching
of new sails, the rigging
of Greek ships to destroy
the citizens of Troy.

Berenice her brother loved,
of all deeds most disapproved,
for she lay at his side,
her girdle's knot untied.

Her sire was Myrrha's only joy,
Semiramis her eldest boy
whom she did destroy.

You've all heard of the Danaids
those most murderous newly-weds
who killed their husbands in their beds.

No better were those dames of Thrace
who did the greatest poet deface;
nor can I relate for shame
the wrong linked with Pasiphae's name.

We've heard about the deeds of Phaedra
and the trickery of Rebecca
and the bane of Deianira;
nor has witnessed any era
since the days of Adam
than Eve a naughtier madam.

No arms ever employed,
no fire, no sea has yet destroyed
as many heroes strong
as fall to woman's tongue.

A girl can make her face
shine brighter in a glass;
she'll set her hair and know
how to make it flow;
she'll prink and preen until
she's trimmed with weapons ill
and ready for the kill.

She'll use the wanton gesture,
and languorous eye corner
and each lascivious move
to kill a man with love.

And when comes the moment
for her to give consent,
to avoid the name
of being too easy game,
she'll weep throughout the skirmish
and yet laugh at the finish.

Her bosom she devests,
the groove between her breasts
will fill the eyes with bane
and make you lust again.
It's dangerous for lads
to know her tricks and fads.

For they are the sea monsters,
they are the deep sea dangers,
the ubiquitous destroyers;
for there's no town or city,
temple or cemetery,
no island and no country,

no meadow or mountain side,
no land or ocean wide,
but there bad girls abide.

They are doomed with the art
which the fates impart
of turning men to stone
with a glance alone.
So young and old take care,
don't fall into love's snare.

Sitting on mountain sward
this satire from a bard
of honeyed muse I heard,
and in the shepherds' cote
I got it all by rote.

Anon
From HATEFUL OLD AGE (9th century Welsh)

Before my back was bent I was eloquent:
For wonders men acclaimed me,
And Argoed's men maintained me.

Before my back was bent I was confident:
A guest at wassails hailed
In Powys paradise of Wales.

Before my back was bent I was eminent
Of mien. My warspear led the attack;
Now bowbacked, downbent, trouble-racked.

Wooden staff, it is autumn
Brown the bracken, the stubble yellow;
What once I loved I've said farewell to.

Wooden staff, it is winter
Men are loud-tongued over their drink;
None puts in at my bed's brink.

Wooden staff, it is spring.
Cuckoos are hidden, clear their plaintive call;
Girls have no use for me at all.

Wooden staff, it is early summer.
Brown the furrow, curly the young corn;
The sight of your crook makes me groan.

This leaf by the wind rolled,
Alas for its destiny.
Born this year: already old.

What I loved as a lad I now curse:
A girl, a stranger, a young horse;
With none of them can I stay the course.

Four ills, of all my hates the chief,
Are met in me together:
Coughing, old age, sickness, grief.

I'm senile, lonely, twisted and cold
After the bed of desire. I'm galled
With misery. My back's thrice-snarled.

No girl wants me, no friend haunts me,
Age daunts and enwalls me.
Ah Death, why don't you call me?

Wretched the doom for Llywarch, doomed
The night he left the womb:
Toil upon toil, long pain, unbroken gloom.

Anon
KING JOHN AND THE ABBOT OF CANTERBURY

An ancient story I'll tell you anon
Of a notable prince, that was called King John;
And he ruled England with maine and with might,
For he did great wrong, and maintain'd little right.

And I'll tell you a story, a story so merrye,
Concerning the Abbot of Canterburye;
How, for his house-keeping and high renowne,
They rode poste for him to fair London towne.

An hundred men, the King did heare say,
The Abbot kept in his house every day;
And fifty golde chaynes, without any doubt,
In velvet coates waited the Abbot about.

'How now, Father Abbot, I heare it of thee
Thou keepest a farre better house than mee,
And for thy house-keeping and high renowne,
I feare thou work'st treason against my crown.' –

'My liege,' quo' the Abbot, 'I would it were knowne,
I never spend nothing, but what is my owne;
And I trust your Grace will doe me no deere
For spending of my owne true-gotten geere.'

'Yes, yes, Father Abbot, thy fault it is highe,
And now for the same thou needest must dye;
For except thou canst answer me questions three,
Thy head shall be smitten from thy bodie.

'And first, ' quo' the King, 'when I'm in this stead,
With my crowne of golde so faire on my head,
Among all my liege-men so noble of birthe,
Thou must tell me to one penny what I am worthe.

'Secondlye, tell me, without any doubt,
How soone I may ride the whole worlde about.
And at the third question thou must not shrinke,
But tell me here truly what I do thinke.' –

'O, these are hard questions for my shallow witt,
Nor I cannot answer your Grace as yet:
But if you will give me but three weekes space,
I'll do my endeavour to answer your Grace.

'Now three weekes space to thee will I give,
And that is the longest time thou hast to live;
For if thou dost not answer my questions three,
Thy lands and thy livings are forfeit to mee.'

Then home rode the Abbot of comfort so cold,
And he mett with his shepheard a-going to fold:
'How now, my lord Abbot, you are welcome home;
What newes do you bring us from good King John?'

'Sad newes, sad newes, shepheard, I must give;
That I have but three days more to live:
For if I do not answer him questions three,
My head will be smitten from my bodie.

'The first is to tell him there in that stead,
With his crowne of golde so fair on his head,
Among all his liege-men so noble of birthe,
To within one penny of what he is worthe.

'The seconde, to tell him, without any doubt,
How soone he may ride this whole worlde about:
And at the third question I must not shrinke,
But tell him there truly what he does thinke.' –

'Now cheare up, sire Abbot, did you never hear yet,
That a fool he may learn a wise man witt?
Lend me horse, and serving-men, and your apparel,
And I'll ride to London to answere your quarrel.'

'Nay frowne not, if it hath bin told unto mee,
I am like your lordship, as ever may bee:
And if you will but lend me your gowne,
There is none shall knowe us at fair London towne.' –

'Now horses and serving-men thou shalt have,
With sumptuous array most gallant and brave,
With crozier, and miter, and rochet, and cope,
Fit to appeare 'fore our Father the Pope.' –

'Now welcome, sire Abbot,' the King he did say,
''Tis well thou'rt come back to keepe thy day;
For and if thou canst answer my questions three,
Thy life and thy living both saved shall bee.

'And first, when thou seest me here in this stead,
With my crown of gold so fair on my head,
Among all my liege-men so noble or birthe,
Tell me to one penny what I am worthe.' –

'For thirty pence our Saviour was sold
Amonge the false Jewes, as I have bin told;
And twenty-nine is the worthe of thee,
For I thinke thou art one penny worser than hee.'

The King he laughed, and swore by St. Bittel,
'I did not thinke I had been worthe so littel!
– Now secondly tell me, without any doubt,
How soone I may ride this whole world about.' –

'You must rise with the sun, and ride with the same,
Until the next morning he riseth againe;
And then your Grace need not make any doubt,
But in twenty-four hours you'll ride it about.'

The King he laughed, and swore by St. Jone,
'I did not think it could be gone so soone!
– Now from the third question you must not shrinke,
But tell me here truly what I do thinke.' –

'Yea, that shall I do, and make your Grace merry:
You thinke I'm the Abbot of Canterburye;
But I'm his poor shepheard, as plain as you may see,
That am come to beg pardon for him and for mee.'

The King he laughed, and swore by the Masse,
'I'll make thee Lord Abbot this day in his place!' –
'Now naye, my liege, be not in such speede,
For alacke I can neither write, ne reade.' –

'Four nobles a weeke, then, I will give thee
For this merry jest thou hast showne unto mee;
And tell the old Abbot when thou comest home,
Thou hast brought him a pardon from good King John.'

Anon
THE LOOM OF TIME

Man's life is laid in the loom of time
    To a pattern he does not see,
While the weavers work and the shuttles fly
    Till the dawn of eternity.

Some shuttles are filled with silver threads
    And some with threads of gold,
While often but the darker hues
    Are all that they may hold.

But the weaver watches with skilful eye
    Each shuttle fly to and fro,
And sees the pattern so deftly wrought
    As the loom moves sure and slow.

God surely planned the pattern:
    Each thread, the dark and fair,
Is chosen by His master skill
    And placed in the web with care.

He only knows its beauty,
  And guides the shuttles which hold
The threads so unattractive,
  As well as the threads of gold.

Not till each loom is silent,
  And the shuttles cease to fly,
Shall God reveal the pattern
  And explain the reason why

The dark threads were as needful
  In the weaver's skilful hand
As the threads of gold and silver
  For the pattern which He planned.

William Allingham
THE FAIRIES

Up the airy mountain,
  Down the rushy glen,
We daren't go a-hunting
  For fear of little men;
Wee folk, good folk,
  Trooping all together;
Green jacket, red cap,
  And white owl's feather!

Down along the rocky shore
  Some make their home,
They live on crispy pancakes
  Of yellow tide-foam;
Some in the reeds
  Of the black mountain lake,
With frogs for their watch-dogs,
  All night awake.

High on the hill-top
   The old King sits;
He is now so old and gray
   He's nigh lost his wits.
With a bridge of white mist
   Columbkill he crosses,
On his stately journeys
   From Slieveleague to Rosses;
Or going up with music
   On cold starry nights
To sup with the Queen
   Of the gay Northern Lights.

They stole little Bridget
   For seven years long;
When she came down again
   Her friends were all gone.
They took her lightly back,
   Between the night and morrow,
They thought that she was fast asleep,
   But she was dead with sorrow.
They have kept her ever since
   Deep within the lake,
On a bed of flag-leaves,
   Watching till she wake.

By the craggy hill-side,
   Through the mosses bare,
They have planted thorn-trees
   For pleasure here and there.
If any man so daring
   As dig them up in spite,
He shall find their sharpest thorns
   In his bed at night.

Up the airy mountain,
   Down the rushy glen,
We daren't go a-hunting

For fear of little men;
Wee folk, good folk,
   Trooping all together;
Green jacket, red cap,
   And white owl's feather!

Anna Bunstone de Bary
UNDER A WILTSHIRE APPLE TREE

Some folks as can afford,
So I've heard say,
Set up a sort of cross
Right in the garden way
To mind 'em of the Lord.
But I, when I do see
Thik apple tree
An' stoopin' limb
All spread wi' moss,
I think of Him
And how He talks wi' me.

I think of God
And how He trod
That garden long ago;
He walked, I reckon, to and fro
And then sat down
Upon the groun'
Or some low limb
What suited Him,
Such as you see
On many a tree,
And on thik very one
Where I at set o' sun
Do sit and talk wi' He.

And, mornings, too, I rise and come
An' sit down where the branch be low;

A bird do sing, a bee do hum,
The flowers in the border blow,
And all my heart's so glad and clear
As pools be when the sun do peer,
As pools a-laughing in the light
When mornin' air is swep' an' bright,
As pools what got all Heaven in sight,
So's my heart's cheer
When He be near.

He never pushed the garden door,
He left no footmark on the floor;
I never heard 'Un stir nor tread
And yet His Hand do bless my head,
And when 'tis time for work to start
I takes Him with me in my heart.
And when I die, pray God I see
At very last thik apple tree
An' stoopin' limb,
And think of Him
And all He been to me.

Thomas Lovell Beddoes
DREAM PEDLARY

If there were dreams to sell,
    What would you buy?
Some cost a passing bell,
    Some a light sigh,
That shakes from Life's fresh crown
Only a rose-leaf down.
If there were dreams to sell,
Merry and sad to tell,
And the crier rang the bell,
    What would you buy?

A cottage lone and still,
      With bowers nigh,
Shadowy, my woes to still,
      Until I die.
Such pearl from Life's fresh crown
Fain would I shake me down.
Were dreams to have at will,
This would best heal my ill,
      This would I buy.

But there were dreams to sell,
      Ill didst thou buy;
Life is a dream, they tell,
      Waking, to die.
Dreaming a dream to prize,
Is wishing ghosts to rise;
      And, if I had the spell
      To call the buried well,
Which one would I?

If there are ghosts to raise,
      What shall I call,
Out of hell's murky haze,
      Heaven's blue pall?
Raise my loved long-lost boy
To lead me to his joy.
      There are no ghosts to raise;
      Out of death lead no ways;
      Vain is the call.

Know'st thou not ghosts to sue?
      No love thou hast.
Else lie, as I will do,
      And breathe thy last.
So out of Life's fresh crown
Fall like a rose-leaf down.
      Thus are the ghosts to woo;
      Thus are all dreams made true,
      Ever to last!

John Betjeman
HOW TO GET ON IN SOCIETY

Phone for the fish-knives, Norman
  As Cook is a little unnerved;
You kiddies have crumpled the serviettes
  And I must have things daintily served.

Are the requisites all in the toilet?
  The frills round the cutlets can wait
Till the girl has replenished the cruets
  And switched on the logs in the grate.

It's ever so close in the lounge, dear,
  But the vestibule's comfy for tea
And Howard is out riding on horseback
  So do come and take some with me.

Now here is a fork for your pastries
  And do use the couch for your feet;
I know what I wanted to ask you –
  If trifle sufficient for sweet?

Milk and then just as it comes, dear?
  I'm afraid the preserve's full of stones;
Beg pardon, I'm soiling the doileys
  With afternoon tea-cakes and scones.

Thomas Blackburn
HOSPITAL FOR DEFECTIVES

By your unnumbered charities
A miracle disclose,
Lord of the Images, whose love,
The eyelid and the rose,
Takes for a language, and today

Tell to me what is said
By these men in a turnip field
And their unleavened bread.

For all things seem to figure out
The stirrings of your heart,
And two men pick the turnips up
And two men pull the cart;
And yet between the four of them
No word is ever said
Because the yeast was not put in
Which makes the human bread.
But three men stare on vacancy
And one man strokes his knees;
What is the meaning to be found
In such dark vowels as these?

Lord of the Images, whose love,
The eyelid and the rose,
Takes for a metaphor, today
Beneath the warder's blows,
The unleavened man did not cry out
Or turn his face away;
Through such men in a turnip field
What is it that you say?

Thomas Bracken
NOT UNDERSTOOD

Not understood. We move along asunder;
Our paths grow wider as the seasons creep
Along the years; we marvel and we wonder
Why life is life. And then we fall asleep –
            Not understood.

Not understood. We gather false impressions,
And hug them closer as the years go by,
Till virtues often seem to us transgressions;
And thus men rise and fall, and live and die –
                    Not understood.

Not understood. Poor souls with stunted vision
Oft measure giants by their narrow gauge;
The poisoned shafts of falsehood and derision
Are oft impelled 'gainst those who mould the age –
                    Not understood.

Not understanding. The secret springs of action
Which lie beneath the surface and the show
Are disregarded; with self-satisfaction
We judge our neighbor, and they often go –
                    Not understood.

Not understood. How trifles often change us!
The thoughtless sentence or the fancied slight
Destroys long years of friendship, and estrange us,
And on our souls there falls a freezing blight –
                    Not understood.

Not understood. How many breasts are aching
For lack of sympathy! Ah, day to day
How many cheerless, lonely hearts are breaking!
How many noble spirits pass away –
                    Not understood.

O God! that men would see a little clearer,
Or judge less harshly where they cannot see;
O God! that men would draw a little nearer
To one another; they'd be nearer Thee –
                    And understood.

Mary Dow Brine
SOMEBODY'S MOTHER

The woman was old and ragged and gray
And bent with the chill of the winter's day.

The street was wet with a recent snow
And the woman's feet were aged and slow.

She stood at the crossing and waited long,
Alone, uncared for, amid the throng.

Of human beings who passed her by
Nor heeded the glance of her anxious eye.

Down the street, with laughter and shout,
Glad in the freedom of 'school let out',

Came the boys like a flock of sheep,
Hailing the snow piled white and deep.

Past the woman so old and gray
Hastened the children on their way.

Nor offered a helping hand to her –
So meek, so timid, afraid to stir

Lest the carriage wheels or the horses' feet
Should crowd her down in the slippery street.

At last came one of the merry troop,
The gayest laddie of all the group;

He paused beside her and whispered low,
'I'll help you cross, if you wish to go.'

Her aged hand on his strong young arm
She placed, and so, without hurt or harm,

He guided the trembling feet along,
Proud that his own were firm and strong.

Then back again to his friends he went,
His young heart happy and well content.

'She's somebody's mother, boys, you know,
For all she's aged and poor and slow,

'And I hope some fellow will lend a hand
To help my mother, you understand,

'If ever she's poor and old and gray,
When her own dear boy is far away.'

And 'somebody's mother' bowed low her head
In her home that night, and the prayer she said

Was 'God be kind to the noble boy,
Who is somebody's son, and pride and joy!'

Emily Brontë
LAST LINES

No coward soul is mine,
No trembler in the world's storm-troubled sphere;
   I see Heaven's glories shine,
And faith shines equal, arming me from fear.

   O God within my breast,
Almighty, ever-present Deity!
   Life – that in me has rest,
As I – undying Life – have power in Thee!

Vain are the thousand creeds
That move men's hearts; unutterably vain;
   Worthless as withered weeds,
Or idlest froth amid the boundless main,

   To waken doubt in one
Holding so fast by Thine Infinity;
   So surely anchored on
The steadfast rock of immortality.

   With wide-embracing love
Thy Spirit animates eternal years,
   Pervades and broods above,
Changes, sustains, dissolves, creates, and rears.

   Though earth and man were gone,
And suns and universes ceased to be,
   And Thou were left alone,
Every existence would exist in Thee.

   There is not room for Death,
Nor atom that his might could render void:
   Thou – Thou art Being and Breath,
And what Thou art may never be destroyed.

Rupert Brooke
THE SOLDIER

If I should die, think only this of me:
   That there's some corner of a foreign field
That is for ever England. There shall be
   In that rich earth a richer dust concealed;
A dust whom England bore, shaped, made aware,
   Gave, once, her flowers to love, her ways to roam,
A body of England's, breathing English air,
   Washed by the rivers, blessed by suns of home.

And think, this heart, all evil shed away,
   A pulse in the eternal mind, no less
      Gives somewhere back the thoughts by England given;
Her sights and sounds; dreams happy as her day;
   And laughter, learnt of friends; and gentleness,
      In hearts at peace, under an English heaven.

Christy Brown
COME SOFTLY TO MY WAKE

Come softly to my wake
on Pavlova feet
at the greying end of day;
into the smoke and heat
enter quietly smiling, quietly unknown
among the garrulous guests
gathered in porter nests
to reminisce and moan;
come not with ornate grief
to desecrate my sleep
but a calm togetherness of hands
quiet as windless sands
and if you must weep
be it for the old quick lust
now lost in dust
only you could shake
from its lair.

Come softly to my wake
and drink and break
the rugged crust
of friendly bread
and weep not for me dead
but lying stupidly there

upon the womanless bed
with a sexless stare
and no thought in my head.

Elizabeth Barrett Browning
A MUSICAL INSTRUMENT

What was he doing, the great god Pan,
   Down in the reeds by the river?
Spreading ruin and scattering ban,
Splashing and paddling with hoofs of a goat,
And breaking the golden lilies afloat
   With the dragon-fly on the river.

He tore out a reed, the great god Pan,
   From the deep cool bed of the river:
The limpid water turbidly ran,
And the broken lilies a-dying lay,
And the dragon-fly had fled away,
   Ere he brought it out of the river.

High on the shore sat the great god Pan,
   While turbidly flowed the river;
And hacked and hewed as a great god can,
With his hard bleak steel at the patient reed,
Till there was not a sign of a leaf indeed
   To prove it fresh from the river.

He cut it short, did the great god Pan
   (How tall it stood in the river!),
Then drew the pith, like the heart of a man,
Steadily from the outside ring,
And notched the poor dry empty thing
   In holes, as he sat by the river.

'This is the way,' laughed the great god Pan,
  (Laughed while he sat by the river),
'The only way, since gods began
To make sweet music, they could succeed.'
Then, dropping his mouth to a hole in the reed,
  He blew in power by the river.

Sweet, sweet, sweet, O Pan!
  Piercing sweet by the river!
Blinding sweet, O great god Pan!
The sun on the hill forgot to die,
And the lilies revived, and the dragon-fly
  Came back to dream on the river.

Yet half a beast is the great god Pan,
  To laugh as he sits by the river,
Making a poet out of a man;
The true gods sigh for the cost and pain –
For the reed which grows nevermore again
  As a reed with the reeds in the river.

Robert Browning
MY LAST DUCHESS

That's my last Duchess painted on the wall,
Looking as if she were alive. I call
That piece a wonder, now: Frà Pandolf's hands
Worked busily a day, and there she stands.
Will't please you sit and look at her? I said
'Frà Pandolf' by design, for never read
Strangers like you that pictured countenance,
The depth and passion of its earnest glance,
But to myself they turned (since none puts by
The curtain I have drawn for you, but I)
And seemed as they would ask me, if they durst,

How such a glance came there; so, not the first
Are you to turn and ask thus. Sir, 'twas not
Her husband's presence only, called that spot
Of joy into the Duchess' cheek: perhaps
Fra Pandolf chanced to say 'Her mantle laps
Over my lady's wrist too much,' or 'Paint
Must never hope to reproduce the faint
Half-flush that dies along her throat': such stuff
Was courtesy, she thought, and cause enough
For calling up that spot of joy. She had
A heart – how shall I say? – too soon made glad,
Too easily impressed; she liked whate'er
She looked on, and her looks went everywhere.
Sir, 'twas all one! My favour at her breast,
The dropping of the daylight in the West,
The bough of cherries some officious fool
Broke in the orchard for her, the white mule
She rode with round the terrace – all and each
Would draw from her alike the approving speech,
Or blush, at least. She thanked men, – good! but thanked
Somehow – I know not how – as if she ranked
My gift of a nine-hundred-years-old name
With anybody's gift. Who'd stoop to blame
This sort of trifling? Even had you skill
In speech – (which I have not) – to make your will
Quite clear to such an one, and say, 'Just this
Or that in you disgusts me; here you miss,
Or there exceed the mark' – and if she let
Herself be lessoned so, nor plainly set
Her wits to yours, forsooth, and made excuse,
– E'en then would be some stooping; and I choose
Never to stoop. Oh sir, she smiled, no doubt,
Whene'er I passed her; but who passed without
Much the same smile? This grew; I gave commands;
Then all smiles stopped together. There she stands
As if alive. Will't please you rise? We'll meet
The company below, then. I repeat,

The Count your master's known munificence
Is ample warrant that no just pretence
Of mine for dowry will be disallowed;
Though his fair daughter's self, as I avowed
At starting, is my object. Nay, we'll go
Together down, sir. Notice Neptune, though,
Taming a sea-horse, thought a rarity,
Which Claus of Innsbruck cast in bronze for me!

John William Burgon
From PEDRA

It seems no work of man's creative hand,
By labour wrought as wavering fancy plann'd,
But from the rock as if by magic grown,
Eternal, silent, beautiful, alone!
Not virgin-white like the old Doric shrine
Where erst Athena held her rites divine;
Not saintly-grey, like many a minster fane,
That crowns the hill, and consecrates the plain;
But rosy-red as if the blush of dawn
That first beheld them were not yet withdrawn;
The hues of youth upon a brow of woe,
Which man deemed old two thousand years ago.
Match me such marvel save in Eastern clime,
A rose-red city half as old as Time.

George Gordon, Lord Byron
THE DESTRUCTION OF SENNACHERIB

The Assyrian came down like the wolf on the fold,
And his cohorts were gleaming in purple and gold;
And the sheen of their spears was like stars on the sea,
When the blue wave rolls nightly on deep Galilee.

Like the leaves of the forest when summer is green,
That host with their banners at sunset were seen:
Like the leaves of the forest when autumn hath blown,
That host on the morrow lay withered and strown.

For the Angel of Death spread his wings on the blast,
And breathed on the face of the foe as he passed:
And the eyes of the sleepers waxed deadly and chill,
And their hearts but once heaved, and for ever grew still!

And there lay the steed with his nostril all wide,
But through it there rolled not the breath of his pride:
And the foam of his gasping lay white on the turf,
And cold as the spray of the rock-beating surf.

And there lay the rider distorted and pale,
With the dew on his brow, and the rust on his mail;
And the tents were all silent, the banners alone,
The lances unlifted, the trumpet unblown.

And the widows of Ashur are loud in their wail,
And the idols are broke in the temple of Baal;
And the might of the Gentile, unsmote by the sword,
Hath melted like snow in the glance of the Lord!

Thomas Campbell
THE HARPER

On the green banks of Shannon, when Sheelah was nigh,
No blithe Irish lad was so happy as I;
No harp like my own could so cheerily play,
And wherever I went was my poor dog Tray.

When at last I was forced from my Sheelah to part,
She said (while the sorrow was big at her heart),
'Oh! remember your Sheelah when far, far away;
And be kind, my dear Pat, to our poor dog Tray.'

Poor dog! he was faithful and kind, to be sure,
And he constantly loved me, although I was poor;
When the sour-looking folk sent me heartless away,
I had always a friend in my poor dog Tray.

When the road was so dark, and the night was so cold,
And Pat and his dog were grown weary and old,
How snugly we slept in my old coat of gray,
And he licked me for kindness – my poor dog Tray.

Though my wallet was scant I remembered his case,
Nor refused my last crust to his pitiful face;
But he died at my feet on a cold winter day,
And I played a sad lament for my poor dog Tray.

Where now shall I go, forsaken and blind?
Can I find one to guide me so faithful and kind?
To my sweet native village, so far, far away,
I can never more return with my poor dog Tray.

William Herbert Carruth
EACH IN HIS OWN TONGUE

A fire mist and a planet –
    A crystal and a cell –
A jellyfish and a saurian,
    And caves where the cave men dwell;
Then a sense of law and beauty,
    And a face turned from the clod –
Some call it Evolution.
    And others call it God.

A haze on the far horizon,
  The infinite, tender sky,
The ripe, rich tint of the cornfields,
  And the wild geese sailing high;
And all over upland and lowland
  The charm of the goldenrod –
Some of us call it Autumn,
  And others call it God.

Like tides on a crescent sea beach,
  When the moon is new and thin,
Into our hearts high yearnings
  Come welling and surging in –
Come from the mystic ocean,
  Whose rim no foot has trod –
Some of us call it Longing,
  And others call it God.

A picket frozen on duty,
  A mother starved for her brood,
Socrates drinking the hemlock,
  And Jesus on the rood;
And millions who, humble and nameless,
  The straight, hard pathway plod –
Some call it Consecration
  And others call it God.

Charles Causley
BALLAD OF THE BREAD MAN

Mary stood in the kitchen
  Baking a loaf of bread.
An angel flew in through the window.
  'We've a job for you,' he said.

'God in his big gold heaven,
   Sitting in his big blue chair,
Wanted a mother for his little son,
   Suddenly saw you there.'

Mary shook and trembled,
   'It isn't true what you say.'
'Don't say that,' said the angel.
   'The baby's on its way.'

Joseph was in the workshop
   Planing a piece of wood.
'The old man's past it,' the neighbours said.
   'That girl's been up to no good.'

'And who was that elegant fellow,'
   They said, 'in the shiny gear?'
The things they said about Gabriel
   Were hardly fit to hear.

Mary never answered,
   Mary never replied,
She kept the information,
   Like the baby, safe inside.

It was election winter.
   They went to vote in town.
When Mary found her time had come
   The hotels let her down.

The baby was born in an annexe
   Next to the local pub.
At midnight, a delegation
   Turned up from the Farmers' Club.

They talked about an explosion
    That made a hole in the sky,
Said they'd been sent to the Lamb & Flag
    To see God come down from on high.

A few days later a bishop
    And a five-star general were seen
With the head of an African country
    In a bullet-proof limousine.

'We've come,' they said, 'with tokens
    For the little boy to choose.'
Told the tale about war and peace
    In the television news.

After them came the soldiers
    With rifle and bomb and gun,
Looking for enemies of the state,
    The family had packed and gone.

When they got back to the village
    The neighbours said, to a man,
'That boy will never be one of us,
    Though he does what he blessed well can.'

He went round to all the people
    A paper crown on his head.
Here is some bread from my father.
    Take, eat, he said.

Nobody seemed very hungry.
    Nobody seemed to care.
Nobody saw the god in himself
    Quietly standing there.

He finished up in the papers.
   He came to a very bad end.
He was charged with bringing the living to life.
   No man was that prisoner's friend.

There's only one kind of punishment
   To fit that kind of a crime
They rigged a trial and shot him dead.
   They were only just in time.

They lifted the young man by the leg,
   They lifted him by the arm,
They locked him in a cathedral
   In case he came to harm.

They stored him safe as water
   Under seven rocks.
One Sunday morning he burst out
   Like a jack-in-the-box.

Through the town he went walking.
   He showed them the holes in his head.
Now do you want any loaves? he cried.
   'Not today,' they said.

Gilbert Keith Chesterton
THE ROLLING ENGLISH ROAD

Before the Roman came to Rye or out to Severn strode,
The rolling English drunkard made the rolling English road.
A reeling road, a rolling road, that rambles round the shire,
And after him the parson ran, the sexton and the squire;
A merry road, a mazy road, and such as we did tread
The night we went to Birmingham by way of Beachy Head.

I knew no harm of Bonaparte and plenty of the Squire,
And for to fight the Frenchman I did not much desire;
But I did bash their baggonest because they came array'd
To straighten out the crooked road an English drunkard
    made,
Where you and I went down the lane with ale-mugs in our
    hands,
The night we went to Glastonbury by way of Goodwin
    Sands.

His sins they were forgiven him; or why do flowers run
Behind him; and the hedges all strengthening in the sun?
The wild thing went from left to right and knew not which
    was which,
But the wild rose was above him when they found him in
    the ditch.
God pardon us, not harden us; we did not see so clear
The night we went to Bannockburn by way of Brighton Pier.

My friends, we will not go again or ape an ancient rage,
Or stretch the folly of our youth to be the shame of age,
But walk with clearer eyes and ears this path that wandereth,
And see undrugg'd in evening light the decent inn of death;
For there is good news yet to hear and fine things to be
    seen,
Before we go to Paradise by way of Kensal Green.

Samuel Taylor Coleridge
KUBLA KHAN

In Xanadu did Kubla Khan
A stately pleasure-dome decree:
Where Alph, the sacred river, ran
Through caverns measureless to man
    Down to a sunless sea.

So twice five miles of fertile ground
With walls and towers were girdled round:
And here were gardens bright with sinuous rills,
Where blossomed many an incense-bearing tree;
And here were forests ancient as the hills
Enfolding sunny spots of greenery.

But oh! that deep romantic chasm which slanted
Down the green hill athwart a cedarn cover!
A savage place! as holy and enchanted
As e'er beneath a waning moon was haunted
By woman wailing for her demon-lover!
And from this chasm, with ceaseless turmoil seething,
As if this earth in fast thick pants were breathing,
A mighty fountain momently was forced:
Amid whose swift half-intermitted burst
Huge fragments vaulted like rebounding hail,
Or chaffy grain beneath the thresher's flail;
And 'mid these dancing rocks at once and ever
It flung up momently the sacred river.
Five miles meandering with a mazy motion
Through wood and dale the sacred river ran,
Then reached the caverns measureless to man,
And sank in tumult to a lifeless ocean:
And 'mid this tumult Kubla heard from far
Ancestral voices prophesying war!

The shadow of the dome of pleasure
Floated midway on the waves;
Where was heard the mingled measure
From the fountain and the caves.
It was a miracle of rare device,
A sunny pleasure-dome with caves of ice!

A damsel with a dulcimer
In a vision once I saw:
It was an Abyssinian maid,

And on her dulcimer she played,
Singing of Mount Abora.
Could I revive within me
Her symphony and song,
To such a deep delight 'twould win me,
That with music loud and long,
I would build that dome in air,
That sunny dome! those caves of ice!
And all who heard should see them there,
And all should cry, Beware! Beware!
His flashing eyes, his floating hair!
Weave a circle round him thrice,
And close your eyes with holy dread,
For he on honey-dew hath fed,
And drunk the milk of Paradise.

Padraic Colum
SHE MOVED THROUGH THE FAIR

My young love said to me, 'My brothers won't mind,
And my parents won't slight you for your lack of kind.'
Then she stepped away from me, and this she did say,
'It will not be long, love, till our wedding day.'

She stepped away from me and she moved through the fair,
And fondly I watched her go here and go there,
Then she went her way homeward with one star awake,
As the swan in the evening moves over the lake.

The people were saying no two were e'er wed
But one had a sorrow that never was said,
And I smiled as she passed with her goods and her gear,
And that was the last that I saw of my dear.

I dreamt it last night that my young love came in,
So softly she entered, her feet made no din;
She came close beside me, and this she did say,
'It will not be long, love, till our wedding day.'

Frances Cornford
PRE-EXISTENCE

I laid me down upon the shore
· And dreamed a little space;
I heard the great waves break and roar
The sun was on my face.

My idle hands and fingers brown
Played with the pebbles grey;
The waves came up, the waves went down,
Both thundering and gay.

The pebbles smooth and salt and round
Were warm upon my hands,
Like little people I had found
Sitting among the sands.

The grains of sand completely small
Soft through my fingers ran;
The sun shone down upon us all,
And so my dream began:

How all of this had been before,
How ages far away
I lay on some forgotten shore
As here I lie today.

The waves came shining up the sands,
  As here today they shine;
And in my pre-Pelasgian hands
  The sand was warm, and fine.

I have forgotten whence I came
  Or where my home might be,
Or by what strange and savage name
  I called that thundering sea.

I only know the sun shone down
  As still it shines today,
And friendly in my fingers brown
  The little pebbles lay.

William Johnson Cory
HERACLITUS

They told me, Heraclitus, they told me you were dead,
They brought me bitter news to hear and bitter tears to shed.
I wept as I remembered how often you and I
Had tired the sun with talking and sent him down the sky.

And now that thou art lying, my dear old Carian guest,
A handful of grey ashes, long, long ago at rest,
Still are thy pleasant voices, thy nightingales, awake;
For Death, he taketh all away, but them he cannot take.

Noël Coward
LIE IN THE DARK AND LISTEN

Lie in the dark and listen
It's clear tonight so they're flying high
Hundreds of them, thousands perhaps
Riding the icy, moonlit sky
Men, machinery, bombs and maps
Altimeters and guns and charts
Coffee, sandwiches, fleece-lined boots
Bones and muscles and minds and hearts
English saplings with English roots
Deep in the earth they've left below
Lie in the dark and let them go
Lie in the dark and listen.

Lie in the dark and listen
They're going over in waves and waves
High above villages, hills and streams,
Country churches and little graves
And little citizens' worried dreams
Very soon they'll have reached the sea
And far below them will lie the bays
And cliffs and sands where they used to be
Taken for summer holidays
Lie in the dark and let them go
Theirs is a world we'll never know
Lie in the dark and listen.

Lie in the dark and listen
City magnates and steel contractors
Factory workers and politicians
Soft hysterical little actors
Ballet dancers, reserved musicians
Safe in your warm civilian beds
Count your profits and count your sheep
Life is passing over your heads

Just turn over and try to sleep
Lie in the dark and let them go
There's one debt you'll forever owe
Lie in the dark and listen.

Ralph Spaulding Cushman
THE SECRET

I met God in the morning
    When my day was at its best,
And His presence came like sunrise,
    Like a glory in my breast.

All day long the Presence lingered,
    All day long He stayed with me,
And we sailed in perfect calmness
    O'er a very troubled sea.

Other ships were blown and battered,
    Other ships were sore distressed,
But the winds that seemed to drive them
    Brought to us a peace and rest.

But I thought of other mornings,
    With a keen remorse of mind,
When I too had loosed the moorings,
    With the Presence left behind.

So I think I know the secret,
    Learned from many a troubled way:
You must seek Him in the morning
    If you want Him through the day!

Emily Dickinson
BECAUSE I COULD NOT STOP FOR DEATH

Because I could not stop for Death –
He kindly stopped for me –
The Carriage held but just Ourselves –
And Immortality.

We slowly drove – He knew no haste
And I had put away
My labor and my leisure too,
For His Civility –

We passed the School, where Children strove
At Recess – in the Ring –
We passed the Fields of Gazing Grain –
We passed the Setting Sun –

Or rather – He passed Us –
The Dews drew quivering and chill –
For only Gossamer, my Gown –
My Tippet – only Tulle –

We paused before a House that seemed
A Swelling of the Ground –
The Roof was scarcely visible –
The Cornice – in the Ground – .

Since then – 'tis Centuries – and yet
Feels shorter than the Day
I first surmised the Horses' Heads
Were toward Eternity –

Ernest Dowson
VITAE SUMMA BREVIS SPEM NOS VETAT INCOHARE LONGAM

They are not long, the weeping and the laughter,
    Love and desire and hate:
I think they have no portion in us after
    We pass the gate.

They are not long, the days of wine and roses:
They are not long, the days of wine and roses:
    Out of a misty dream
Our path emerges for a while, then closes
    Within a dream.

Michael Drayton
THE PARTING

Since there's no help, come let us kiss and part;
Nay, I have done, you get no more of me,
And I am glad, yea, glad with all my heart,
That thus so cleanly I myself can free.
Shake hands for ever, cancel all our vows,
And when we meet at any time again,
Be it not seen in either of our brows
That we one jot of former love retain.
Now at the last gasp of Love's latest breath,
When, his pulse failing, Passion speechless lies,
When Faith is kneeling by his bed of death,
And Innocence is closing up his eyes.
    Now if thou would'st, when all have given him over,
    From death to life thou might'st him yet recover.

John Drinkwater
MOONLIT APPLES

At the top of the house the apples are laid in rows,
And the skylight lets the moonlight in, and those
Apples are deep-sea apples of green. There goes
    A cloud on the moon in the autumn night.
A mouse in the wainscot scratches, and scratches, and then
There is no sound at the top of the house of men
Or mice; and the cloud is blown, and the moon again
    Dapples the apples with deep-sea light.

They are lying in rows there, under the gloomy beams;
On the sagging floor; they gather the silver streams
Out of the moon, those moonlit apples of dreams,
    And quiet is the steep stair under.

In the corridors under there is nothing but sleep.
And stiller than ever on orchard boughs they keep
Tryst with the moon, and deep is the silence, deep
    On moon-washed apples of wonder.

T.S. Eliot
JOURNEY OF THE MAGI

    'A cold coming we had of it,
Just the worst time of the year
For a journey, and such a long journey:
The ways deep and the weather sharp,
The very dead of winter.'
And the camels galled, sore-footed, refractory,
Lying down in the melting snow.
There were times we regretted
The summer palaces on slopes, the terraces,
And the silken girls bringing sherbet.

Then the camel men cursing and grumbling
And running away, and wanting their liquor and women,
And the night-fires going out, and the lack of shelters,
And the cities hostile and the towns unfriendly
And the villages dirty and charging high prices:
A hard time we had of it.
At the end we preferred to travel all night,
Sleeping in snatches,
With the voices singing in our ears, saying
That this was all folly.

Then at dawn we came down to a temperate valley,
Wet, below the snow line, smelling of vegetation,
With a running stream and a water-mill beating the darkness,
And three trees on the low sky.
And an old white horse galloped away in the meadow.
Then we came to a tavern with vine-leaves over the lintel,
Six hands at an open door dicing for pieces of silver,
And feet kicking the empty wine-skins.
But there was no information, and so we continued
And arrived at evening, not a moment too soon
Finding the place; it was (you may say) satisfactory.

All this was a long time ago, I remember,
And I would do it again, but set down
This set down
This: were we led all that way for
Birth or Death? There was a Birth, certainly,
We had evidence and no doubt. I had seen birth and death,
But had thought they were different; this Birth was
Hard and bitter agony for us, like Death, our death.
We returned to our places, these Kingdoms,
But no longer at ease here, in the old dispensation,
With an alien people clutching their gods.
I should be glad of another death.

E. Farmer
LITTLE JIM

The cottage was a thatch'd one,
  The outside old and mean,
Yet everything within that cot
  Was wondrous neat and clean.

The night was dark and stormy,
  The wind was howling wild;
A patient mother knelt beside
  The death bed of her child.

A little worn-out creature,
  His once bright eyes grown dim;
It was a collier's only child,
  They called him Little Jim.

And, oh! to see the briny tears
  Fast hurrying down her cheeks,
As she offer'd up a prayer in thought,
  She was afraid to speak.

Lest she might waken one she loved
  Far better than her life;
For there was all a mother's love
  In that poor collier's wife.

With hands uplifted, see, she kneels,
  Beside the sufferer's bed;
And prays that He will spare her boy,
  And take herself instead.

She gets her answer from the child,
  Soft fell these words from him,
'Mother, the angels do so smile,
  And beckon Little Jim.

I have no pain, dear mother, now,
    But oh! I am so dry;
Just moisten poor Jim's lips again,
    And mother, don't you cry.'

With gentle, trembling haste she held
    The tea-cup to his lips;
He smiled to thank her, as he took
    Three tiny little sips.

'Tell father when he comes from work,
    I said "good-night" to him;
And, mother, now I'll go to sleep,'
    Alas, poor Little Jim.

She saw that he was dying –
    The child she loved so dear
Had uttered the last words that she
    Might ever hope to hear.

The cottage door was opened
    The collier's step is heard,
The father and the mother meet,
    Yet neither speak a word.

He knew that all was over,
    He knew his child was dead;
He took the candle in his hand,
    And walked towards the bed.

His quivering lips gave token
    Of the grief he'd fain conceal;
And see his wife has joined him –
    The stricken couple kneel.

With hearts bowed down with sadness
    They humbly ask of Him,
In heaven, once more to meet again.
    Their own poor Little Jim.

John Meade Falkner
AFTER TRINITY

We have done with dogma and divinity
    Easter and Whitsun past,
The long, long Sundays after Trinity
    Are with us at last;
The passionless Sundays after Trinity,
    Neither feast-day nor fast.

Christmas comes with plenty,
    Lent spreads out its pall,
But these are five and twenty,
    The longest Sundays of all;
The placid Sundays after Trinity,
    Wheat-harvest, fruit-harvest, Fall.

Spring with its burst is over,
    Summer has had its day.
The scented grasses and clover
    Are cut, and dried into hay;
The singing-birds are silent,
    And the swallows flown away.

Post pugnam pausa fiet;
    Lord, we have made our choice;
In the stillness of autumn quiet,
    We have heard the still, small voice.
We have sung *Oh where shall Wisdom ?*
    Thick paper, folio, Boyce.

Let it not all be sadness,
  Not *omnia vanitas,*
Stir up a little gladness
  To lighten the *Tibi cras*;
Send us that little summer
  That comes with Martinmas.

When still the cloudlet dapples
  The windless cobalt-blue,
And the scent of gathered apples
  Fills all the store-rooms through,
The gossamer silvers the bramble,
  The lawns are gemmed with dew.

An end of tombstone Latinity,
  Stir up sober mirth,
Twenty-fifth after Trinity,
  Kneel with the listening earth,
Behind the Advent trumpets
  They are singing Emmanuel's birth.

Rachel Field
GYPSIES

Last night the gypsies came –
  Nobody knows from where.
Where they've gone to nobody knows,
  And nobody seems to care!

Between the trees on the old swamp road
  I saw them round their fire:
Tattered children and dogs that barked
  As the flames leaped high and higher;
There were black-eyed girls in scarlet shawls,

Old folk wrinkled with years,
Men with handkerchiefs round their throats
  And silver loops in their ears.
Ragged and red like maple leaves
  When frost comes in the fall,
The gypsies stayed but a single night;
  In the morning gone were all –
Never a shaggy gypsy dog,
  Never a gypsy child;
Only a burnt-out gypsy fire
  Where danced that band so wild.

All gone and away,
  Who knows where?
Only the wind that sweeps
  Maple branches bare.

James Elroy Flecker
WAR SONG OF THE SARACENS

We are they who come faster than fate: we are they who ride
    early or late:
We storm at your ivory gate: Pale Kings of the Sunset,
    beware!
Not on silk nor in samet we lie, not in curtained solemnity
    die
Among women who chatter and cry, and children who
    mumble a prayer.
But we sleep by the ropes of the camp, and we rise with a
    shout, and we tramp
With the sun or the moon for a lamp, and the spray of the
    wind in our hair.

From the lands where the elephants are, to the forts of
    Merou and Balghar,
Our steel we have brought and our star to shine on the ruins
    of Rum.
We have marched from the Indus to Spain, and by God we
    will go there again;
We have stood on the shore of the plain where the Waters of
    Destiny boom.
A mart of destruction we made a Jalula where men were
    afraid,
For death was a difficult trade, and the sword was a broker
    of doom;

And the Spear was a Desert Physician who cured not a few
    of ambition,
And drave not a few to perdition with medicine bitter and
    strong:
And the shield was a grief to the fool and as bright as a
    desolate pool,
And as straight as the rock of Stamboul when their cavalry
    thundered along:
For the coward was drowned with the brave when our battle
    sheered up like a wave,
And the dead to the desert we gave, and the glory to God in
    our song.

Robin Flower
TIR NA N-OG

I heard the summer calling across great breadths of sea
In the landwind and the seawind and the wind of gramarie;
For the seawind speaks in thunder and the landwind whis-
    pers low,
But the little wind of faery you scarce can hear it blow.

But listen, listen, listen and you shall hear afar
A low and lovely murmur like the singing of a star;
But listen, listen, listen, till all things fade and fall
And the lone and luring music is master over all.

And you shall hear it chanting in one triumphant chime
Of the life that lives for ever and the fugitives of time
Beyond the green land's border and the washing wastes of
    sea
In the world beyond the world's end, where nothing is but
    glee.

The magic waters gird it, and skies of laughing blue
Keep always faith with summer and summer still is true;
There is no end of dancing and sweet unceasing song,
And eyes to eyes make answer and love with love grows
    strong.

But close your ears and silence the crying of your heart,
Lest in the world of mortals you walk a man apart;
For O! I heard the music and answered to the call,
And the landwind mocks my longing and the seawind
    saddens all.

St Francis of Assisi
A PRAYER

Lord make me an
  instrument of Thy peace.
  Where there is hatred,
  Let me sow Love;
  Where there is injury,
  Let me sow pardon;
  Where there is doubt, faith;
  Where there is despair, hope;
Where there is darkness, light;
Where there is sadness, joy.

(Amen)

Robert Frost
STOPPING BY WOODS ON A SNOWY EVENING

Whose woods these are I think I know.
His house is in the village though;
He will not see me stopping here
To watch his woods fill up with snow.

My little horse must think it queer
To stop without a farmhouse near
Between the woods and frozen lake
The darkest evening of the year.

He gives his harness bells a shake
To ask if there is some mistake.
The only other sound's the sweep
Of easy wind and downy flake.

The woods are lovely, dark and deep.
But I have promises to keep,
And miles to go before I sleep,
And miles to go before I sleep.

Robert Graves
WELSH INCIDENT

'But that was nothing to what things came out
From the sea-caves of Criccieth yonder.'
'What were they? Mermaids? Dragons? Ghosts?'
'Nothing at all of any things like that.'
'What were they, then?'
                              'All sorts of queer things,
Things never seen or heard or written about,
Very strange, un-Welsh, utterly peculiar
Things. Oh, solid enough they seemed to touch,
Had anyone dared it. Marvellous creation,
All various shapes and sizes, and no sizes,
All new, each perfectly unlike his neighbour,
Though all came moving slowly out together.'
'Describe just one of them.'
                              'I am unable.'
'What were their colours?'
                              'Mostly nameless colours,
Colours you'd like to see; but one was puce
Or perhaps more like crimson, but not purplish
Some had no colour.'
                              'Tell me, had they legs?'
'Not a leg nor foot among them that I saw.'
'But did these things come out in any order?
What o'clock was it? What was the day of the week?
Who else was present? How was the weather?'
'I was coming to that. It was half-past three
On Easter Tuesday last. The sun was shining.

The Harlech Silver Band played *Marchog Jesu*
On thirty-seven shimmering instruments,
collecting for Caernarvon's (Fever) Hospital Fund.
The populations of Pwllheli, Criccieth,
Portmadoc, Borth, Tremadoc, Penrhyndeudraeth,
Were all assembled. Criccieth's mayor addressed them
First in good Welsh and then in fluent English,
Twisting his fingers in his chain of office,
Welcoming the things. They came out on the sand,
Not keeping time to the band, moving seaward
Silently at a snail's pace. But at last
The most odd, indescribable thing of all,
Which hardly one man there could see for wonder,
Did something recognizably a something.'
'Well, what?'
                    'It made a noise.'
                                        'A frightening noise?'
'No, no.'
   'A musical noise? A noise of scuffling?'
'No, but a very loud, respectable noise –
Like groaning to oneself on Sunday morning
In Chapel, close before the second psalm.'
'What did the mayor do?'
                              'I was coming to that.'

Joyce Grenfell
TIME

When I was a girl there was always time,
There was always time to spare.
There was always time to sit in the sun;
And we were never done
With lazing and flirting,
And doing our embroidery,
And keeping up our memory books,

And brushing our hair,
And writing little notes,
And going on picnics,
And dancing, dancing, dancing, dancing –
When I was a girl there was always time to waste.

Thank the Lord.

When I was a young woman there was always time,
There was always time to spare.
There was always time to walk in the sun,
And we were never done
With going to weddings,
Our own and our friends',
And going to parties,
Away at weekends,
And having our children
and bringing them up,
And talking, talking, talking, talking –
When I was a young woman there was always time to enjoy
        things.

Thank the Lord.

And when I was an elderly woman there was no more time,
There was no more time to spare.
There was no more time to sit in the sun,
For we were never done
With answering the telephone,
And looking at the TV,
And doing baby-sitting,
And talking to our friends,
And shopping, shopping, shopping, shopping,
And washing-up, washing-up, washing-up,
Writing letters, writing letters
Rushing, rushing, rushing,
And we were always hurried,

And we were never bored.
When I was an elderly woman
There was never time to think.

Thank the Lord.

But now I'm an old old woman,
So I want the last word:
There is no such thing as time –
Only this very minute
And I'm in it.

Thank the Lord.

George Herbert
LOVE (III)

Love bade me welcome; yet my soul drew back,
            Guilty of dust and sin.
But quick-eyed Love, observing me grow slack
            From my first entrance in,
Drew nearer to me, sweetly questioning
            If I lack'd anything.

'A guest,' I answer'd, 'worthy to be here:'
            Love said, 'You shall be he.'
'I, the unkind, ungrateful? Ah, my dear,
            I cannot look on thee.'
Love took my hand and smiling did reply,
            'Who made the eyes but I?'

'Truth, Lord; but I have marr'd them: let my shame
            Go where it doth deserve.'
'And know you not,' says Love, 'Who bore the blame?'
            'My dear, then I will serve.'
'You must sit down,' says Love, 'and taste my meat.'
            So I did sit and eat.

Ralph Hodgson
TIME, YOU OLD GIPSY MAN

Time, you old gipsy man,
   Will you not stay,
Put up your caravan
   Just for one day?

All things I'll give you,
Will you be my guest,
Bells for your jennet
Of silver the best,
Goldsmiths shall beat you
A great golden ring,
Peacocks shall bow to you,
Little boys sing,
Oh, the sweet girls will
Festoon you with may,
Time, you old gipsy,
Why hasten away?

Last week in Babylon,
Last night in Rome,
Morning, and in the crush
Under Paul's dome,
Under Paul's dial
You tighten your rein –
Only a moment,
And off once again;
Off to some city
Now blind in the womb,
Off to another
Ere that's in the tomb.

Time, you old gipsy man,
   Will you not stay,
Put up your caravan
   Just for one day?

James Hogg
A BOY'S SONG

Where the pools are bright and deep,
Where the grey trout lies asleep,
Up the river and over the lea,
That's the way for Billy and me.

Where the blackbird sings the latest,
Where the hawthorn blooms the sweetest,
Where the nestlings chirp and flee,
That's the way for Billy and me.

Where the mowers mow the cleanest,
Where the hay lies thick and greenest,
There to track the homeward bee,
That's the way for Billy and me.

Where the hazel bank is steepest,
Where the shadow falls the deepest,
Where the clustering nuts fall free,
That's the way for Billy and me.

Why the boys should drive away
Little sweet maidens from the play,
Or love to banter and fight so well,
That's the thing I never could tell.

But this I know, I love to play
Through the meadow, among the hay;
Up the water and over the lea,
That's the way for Billy and me.

Thomas Hood
I REMEMBER, I REMEMBER

I remember, I remember,
   The house where I was born,
The little window where the sun
   Came peeping in at morn;
He never came a wink too soon,
   Nor brought too long a day,
But now, I often wish the night
   Had borne my breath away.

I remember, I remember,
   The roses, red and white;
The violets, and the lily-cups,
   Those flowers made of light!
The lilacs where the robin built,
   And where my brother set
The laburnum on his birthday –
   The tree is living yet!

I remember, I remember,
   Where I was used to swing;
And thought the air must rush as fresh
   To swallows on the wing:
My spirit flew in feathers then,
   That is so heavy now,
And summer pools could hardly cool
   The fever on my brow!

I remember, I remember,
   The fir trees dark and high;
I used to think their slender tops
   Were close against the sky:
It was a childish ignorance,
   But now 'tis little joy
To know I'm farther off from Heav'n
   Than when I was a boy.

Gerard Manley Hopkins
THE WINDHOVER

To Christ our Lord

I caught this morning morning's minion, king-
   dom of daylight's dauphin, dapple-dawn-drawn Falcon, in
      his riding
Of the rolling level underneath him steady air, and striding
High there, how he rung upon the rein of a wimpling wing
In his ecstasy! then off, off forth on swing,
   As a skate's heel sweeps smooth on a bow-bend: the hurl
      and gliding
   Rebuffed the big wind. My heart in hiding
Stirred for a bird, – the achieve of, the mastery of the thing!

Brute beauty and valour and act, oh, air, pride, plume, here
   Buckle! AND the fire that breaks from thee then, a billion
Times told lovelier, more dangerous, O my chevalier!

No wonder of it: shéer plód makes plough down sillion
Shine, and blue-bleak embers, ah my dear,
   Fall, gall themselves, and gash gold-vermilion.

Richard Monckton Milnes, Lord Houghton
GOOD NIGHT AND GOOD MORNING

A fair little girl sat under a tree,
Sewing as long as her eyes could see;
Then smoothed her work, and folded it right,
And said, 'Dear work, Good Night! Good Night!'

Such a number of rooks came over her head,
Crying, 'Caw, caw!' on their way to bed;
She said, as she watched their curious flight,
'Little black things, Good Night! Good Night!'

The horses neighed, and the oxen lowed;
The sheep's 'Bleat! bleat!' came over the road;
All seeming to say with a quiet delight,
'Good little girl, Good Night! Good Night!'

She did not say to the sun, 'Good Night!'
Though she saw him there like a ball of light;
For she knew he had God's time to keep
All over the world, and never could sleep.

The tall pink fox-glove bowed his head –
The violets curtsied and went to bed;
And good little Lucy tied up her hair,
And said, on her knees, her favourite prayer.

And while on her pillow she softly lay
She knew nothing more till again it was day:
And all things said to the beautiful sun,
'Good Morning! Good Morning! our work is begun!'

A.E. Housman
BREDON HILL
From *A Shropshire Lad*

In summertime on Bredon
    The bells they sound so clear;
Round both the shires they ring them
    In steeples far and near,
    A happy noise to hear.

Here of a Sunday morning
    My love and I would lie,
And see the coloured counties,
    And hear the larks so high
    About us in the sky.

The bells would ring to call her
  In valleys miles away:
'Come all to church, good people;
  Good people, come and pray.'
  But here my love would stay.

And I would turn and answer
  Among the springing thyme,
'Oh, peal upon our wedding,
  And we will hear the chime,
  And come to church in time.'

But when the snows at Christmas
  On Bredon top were strown,
My love rose up so early
  And stole out unbeknown
  And went to church alone.

They tolled the one bell only,
  Groom there was none to see,
The mourners followed after,
  And so to church went she,
  And would not wait for me.

The bells they sound on Bredon,
  And still the steeples hum.
'Come all to church, good people,' –
  Oh, noisy bells, be dumb;
  I hear you, I will come.

Leigh Hunt
JENNY KISSED ME

Jenny kiss'd me when we met,
   Jumping from the chair she sat in;
Time, you thief, who love to get
   Sweets into your list, put that in!
Say I'm weary, say I'm sad,
   Say that health and wealth have miss'd me,
Say I'm growing old, but add,
   Jenny kiss'd me.

John Keats
TO AUTUMN

Season of mists and mellow fruitfulness,
   Close bosom-friend of the maturing sun;
Conspiring with him how to load and bless
   With fruit the vines that round the thatch-eaves run;
To bend with apples the mossed cottage-trees,
   And fill all fruit with ripeness to the core;
      To swell the gourd, and plump the hazel shells
   With a sweet kernel; to set budding more,
And still more, later flowers for the bees,
Until they think warm days will never cease,
      For Summer has o'er-brimmed their clammy cells.

Who hath not seen thee oft amid thy store?
   Sometimes whoever seeks abroad may find
Thee sitting careless on a granary floor,
   Thy hair soft-lifted by the winnowing wind;
Or on a half-reaped furrow sound asleep,
   Drowsed with the fume of poppies, while thy hook
      Spares the next swath and all its twinèd flowers:

And sometimes like a gleaner thou dost keep
Steady thy laden head across a brook;
Or by a cider-press, with patient look,
    Thou watchest the last oozings, hours by hours.

Where are the songs of Spring? Ay, where are they?
    Think not of them, thou hast thy music too –
While barrèd clouds bloom the soft-dying day,
    And touch the stubble-plains with rosy hue;
Then in a wailful choir the small gnats mourn
    Among the river sallows, borne aloft
        Or sinking as the light wind lives or dies;
    And full-grown lambs loud bleat from hilly bourn;
Hedge-crickets sing; and now with treble soft
The red-breast whistles from a garden-croft;
    And gathering swallows twitter in the skies.

Rudyard Kipling
THE WAY THROUGH THE WOODS

They shut the road through the woods
Seventy years ago.
Weather and rain have undone it again,
And now you would never know
There was once a road through the woods
Before they planted the trees.
It is underneath the coppice and heath
And the thin anemones.
Only the keeper sees
That, where the ring-dove broods,
And the badgers roll at ease,
There was once a road through the woods.

Yet, if you enter the woods
Of a summer evening late,
When the night-air cools on the trout-ringed pools
Where the otter whistles his mate,
(They fear not men in the woods,
Because they see so few.)
You will hear the beat of a horse's feet,
And the swish of a skirt in the dew,
Steadily cantering through
The misty solitudes,
As though they perfectly knew
The old lost road through the woods . . .
But there is no road through the woods.

C.S. Lewis
THE LATE PASSENGER

The sky was low, the sounding rain was falling dense and
    dark,
And Noah's sons were standing at the window of the Ark.

The beasts were in, but Japhet said, 'I see one creature more
Belated and unmated there come knocking at the door.'

'Well let him knock, said Ham, 'Or let him drown or learn to
    swim.
We're overcrowded as it is; we've got no room for him.'

'And yet it knocks, how terribly it knocks,' said Shem, 'Its
    feet
Are hard as horn – but oh the air that comes from it is sweet.'

'Now hush,' said Ham, 'You'll waken Dad, and once he
    comes to see

What's at the door, it's sure to mean more work for you and
    me.'

Noah's voice came roaring from the darkness down below,
'Some animal is knocking. Take it in before we go.'

Ham shouted back, and savagely he nudged the other two,
'That's only Japhet knocking down a brad-nail in his shoe.'

Said Noah, 'Boys, I hear a noise that's like a horse's hoof.'
Said Ham, 'Why, that's the dreadful rain that drums upon the
    roof.'

Noah tumbled up on deck and out he put his head;
His face went grey, His knees were loosed, he tore his beard
    and said,

'Look, look! It would not wait. It turns away. It takes its
    flight.
Fine work you've made of it, my sons, between you all
    tonight!

'Even if I could outrun it now, it would not turn again
- Not now. Our great discourtesy has earned its high disdain.

'Oh noble and unmated beast, my sons were all unkind;
In such a night what stable and what manger will you find?

'Oh golden hoofs, oh cataracts of mane, oh nostrils wide
With indignation! Oh the neck wave-arched, the lovely
    pride!

'Oh long shall be the furrows ploughed across the hearts of
    men
Before it comes to stable and to manger once again,

'And dark and crooked all the ways in which our race shall

walk,
And shrivelled all their manhood like a flower with broken
   stalk,

'And all the world, oh Ham, may curse the hour when you
   were born
Because of you the Ark must sail without the Unicorn.'

Henry Wadsworth Longfellow
THE SLAVE'S DREAM

Beside the ungathered rice he lay,
   His sickle in his hand;
His breast was bare, his matted hair
   Was buried in the sand.
Again, in the mist and shadow of sleep,
   He saw his Native Land.

Wide through the landscape of his dreams
   The lordly Niger flowed;
Beneath the palm-trees on the plain
   Once more a king he strode;
And heard the tinkling caravans
   Descend the mountain-road.

He saw once more his dark-eyed Queen
   Among her children stand;
They clasped his neck, they kissed his cheeks,
   They held him by the hand! –
A tear burst from the sleeper's lids
   And fell into the sand.

And then at furious speed he rode
   Along the Niger's bank;
His bridle-reins were golden chains,

And, with a martial clank,
At each leap he could feel his scabbard of steel
  Smiting his stallion's flank.

Before him, like a blood-red flag,
  The bright flamingoes flew;
From morn till night he followed their flight,
O'er plains where the tamarind grew,
  Till he saw the roofs of Caffre huts,
  And the ocean rose to view.

At night he heard the lion roar,
  And the hyena scream,
And the river-horse, as he crushed the reeds
  Beside some hidden stream;
And it passed, like a glorious roll of drums,
  Through the triumph of his dream.

The forests, with their myriad tongues,
  Shouted of liberty;
And the Blast of the Desert cried aloud,
  With a voice so wild and free,
That he started in his sleep and smiled
  At their tempestuous glee.

He did not feel the driver's whip
  Nor the burning heat of day;
For Death had illumined the Land of Sleep,
  And his lifeless body lay
A worn-out fetter, that the soul
  Had broken and thrown away !

Edward Lowbury
THE LAST DAY

And God said 'Let there be Hate', and there was Hate:
For now, having tried in vain
To breathe Love, as once He had breathed Life,
Into all these creatures,
He saw the game was up.
'Peradventure there be fifty righteous . . .
Wilt Thou destroy, and not spare the place?'
And He said 'For the sake of ten
I will not destroy it.' –

　　　　　But now,
Having stripped the Tree of Knowledge bare,
Man had outrun such grace:
If ten made up their minds
To destroy the city – or, for that matter, the world –
Ten million righteous could do nothing to save it.

So God divided those whom once He joined;
And they rose, and in His name
Blew out the brains of children
And taught children to kill,
In the Lord's name, in a still beautiful country;
In spite of hideous warnings,
The strong trampled the weak,
Sneering in triumph over their confusion,
Madness possessed illiterate kings
To use the last weapon.

And judgement fell upon them,
Blacked out the morning sun from the sixth hour,
And there was darkness over all the earth,

But at midnight the sky
Grew brighter than a thousand suns,
And the evening
And the morning
Were the last day.

Phyllis McCormack
LOOK CLOSER

What do you see, nurses, what do you see?
Are you thinking, when you are looking at me,
A crabbit old woman, not very wise,
Uncertain of habit, with far away eyes,
Who dribbles her food, and makes no reply,
When you say in a loud voice; 'I do wish you'd try',
Who seems not to notice the things that you do,
And forever is losing a stocking or shoe,
Who, quite unresisting, lets you do as you will
With bathing and feeding, the long day to fill?
Is that what you're thinking, is that what you see?
Then open your eyes, you're not looking at me.
I'll tell you who I am, as I sit here so still,
As I move at your bidding, as I eat at your will,
I'm a small child of ten, with a father and mother,
Brothers and sisters, who love one another,
A young girl of sixteen with wings on her feet,
Dreaming that soon a true lover she'll meet;
A bride now at twenty – my heart gives a leap,
Remembering the vows that I promised to keep;
At twenty-five now I have young of my own,
Who need me to build a secure, happy home;
A woman of thirty, my young now grow fast,
Bound to each other with ties that should last;
At forty my young sons will soon all be gone,
But my man stays beside me to see I don't mourn;
At fifty once more babies play round my knee;

Again we know children, my loved one and me.
Dark days are upon me, my husband is dead.
I look at the future, I shudder with dread,
For my young are all busy, with young of their own,
And I think of the years and the love that I've known.
I'm an old woman now and nature is cruel,
'Tis her jest to make old age look like a fool.
The body it crumbles, grace and vigour depart,
There now is a stone where I once had a heart.
But inside this old carcase a young girl still dwells,
And now and again my battered heart swells.
I remember the joys, I remember the pain,
And I'm loving and living life over again.

I think of the years, all too few – gone too fast,
And accept the stark fact that nothing can last.
So open your eyes, nurses, open and see,
Not a crabbit old woman, look closer – see ME.

John McCrae
IN FLANDERS FIELDS

In Flanders fields the poppies blow
Between the crosses, row on row,
    That mark our place; and in the sky
    The larks, still bravely singing, fly
Scarce heard amid the guns below.

We are the Dead. Short days ago
We lived, felt dawn, saw sunset glow,
    Loved and were loved, and now we lie
    In Flanders fields.

Take up our quarrel with the foe:
To you from failing hands we throw
   The torch; be yours to hold it high.
   If ye break faith with us who die
We shall not sleep, though poppies grow
    In Flanders fields.

Charles Mackay
TUBAL CAIN

Old Tubal Cain was a man of might
   In the days when earth was young:
By the fierce red light of his furnace bright
   The strokes of his hammer rung;
And he lifted high his brawny hand
   On the iron glowing clear,
Till the sparks rush'd out in scarlet showers,
   As he fashion'd the sword and spear.
And he sang – 'Hurra for my handiwork!
   Hurra for the Spear and Sword!
Hurra for the hand that shall wield them well,
   For he shall be king and lord!'

To Tubal Cain came many a one,
   As he wrought by his roaring fire,
And each one pray'd for a strong steel blade
   As the crown of his desire;
And he made them weapons sharp and strong,
   Till they shouted loud for glee,
And gave him gifts of pearls and gold,
   And spoils of the forest free.
And they sang – 'Hurra for Tubal Cain,
   Who hath given us strength anew!
Hurra for the smith, hurra for the fire,
   And hurra for the metal true!'

But a sudden change came o'er his heart
   Ere the setting of the sun,
And Tubal Cain was fill'd with pain
   For the evil he had done;
He saw that men, with rage and hate,
   Made war upon their kind,
That the land was red with the blood they shed
   In their lust for carnage, blind.
And he said – 'Alas! that ever I made,
   Or that skill of mine should plan,
The spear and the sword for men whose joy
   Is to slay their fellow-man!'

And for many a day old Tubal Cain
   Sat brooding o'er his woe;
And his hand forebore to smite the ore,
   And his furnace smoulder'd low.
But he rose at last with a cheerful face,
   And a bright courageous eye,
And bared his strong right arm for work,
   While the quick flames mounted high.
And he sang – 'Hurra for my handiwork!'
   And the red sparks lit the air;
'Not alone for the blade was the bright steel made;'
   And he fashion'd the First Ploughshare!

And men, taught wisdom from the Past,
   In friendship join'd their hands,
Hung the sword in the hall, the spear on the wall,
   And plough'd the willing lands,
And sang – 'Hurra for Tubal Cain!
   Our stanch good friend is he;
And for the ploughshare and the plough
   To him our praise shall be.
But while Oppression lifts its head,
   Or a tyrant would be lord,
Though we may thank him for the Plough,
   We'll never forget the Sword!'

Irene McLeod
LONE DOG

I'm a lean dog, a keen dog, a wild dog, and lone;
I'm a rough dog, a tough dog, hunting on my own;
I'm a bad dog, a mad dog, teasing silly sheep;
I love to sit and bay the moon, to keep fat souls from sleep.

I'll never be a lap dog, licking dirty feet,
A sleek dog, a meek dog, cringing for my meat;
Not for me the fireside, the well-filled plate,
But shut door, and sharp stone, and cuff, and kick, and hate.

Not for me the other dogs, running by my side;
Some have run a short while, but none of them would bide,
O mine is still the lone trail, the hard trail, the best,
Wide wind, and wild stars, and the hunger of the quest!

Louis MacNeice
MEETING POINT

Time was away and somewhere else,
There were two glasses and two chairs
And two people with the one pulse
(Somebody stopped the moving stairs):
Time was away and somewhere else.

And they were neither up nor down,
The stream's music did not stop
Flowing through heather, limpid brown,
Although they sat in a coffee shop
And they were neither up nor down.

The bell was silent in the air
Holding its inverted poise –
Between the clang and clang a flower,
A brazen calyx of no noise:
The bell was silent in the air.

The camels crossed the miles of sand
That stretched around the cups and plates;
The desert was their own, they planned
To portion out the stars and dates:
The camels crossed the miles of sand.

Time was away and somewhere else.
The waiter did not come, the clock
Forgot them and the radio waltz
Came out like water from a rock:
Time was away and somewhere else.

Her fingers flicked away the ash
That bloomed again in tropic trees:
Not caring if the markets crash
When they had forests such as these,
Her fingers flicked away the ash.

God or whatever means the Good
Be praised that time can stop like this,
That what the heart has understood
Can verify in the body's peace
God or whatever means the Good

Time was away and she was here
And life no longer what it was,
The bell was silent in the air
And all the room a glow because
Time was away and she was here.

Frank Mansell
SEE THESE HANDS

See these hands folded now,
Hands that wrought for so many,
Tended and tidied a family,
Soothed them and calmed them,
Fed, clothed and reared them
Almost on nothing.

See these hands resting,
That in the old hard days
Picked blackberries for pennies
And gathered dry sticks in bundles,
In dim March days I scarcely remember
When beech woods were a mystery
And fox cubs played among daffodils.

See these hands resting,
That raked hay in the fields
Of a summer coloured with butterflies,
That brought tea and sandwiches
To tired men at harvest,
And scattered wheat and Argentinian maize
To hungry hens.

See these diligent hands, hands never still,
Hands they have folded now,
Hands that are resting,
That will never be active again,
Long though I kneel for their blessing.

Andrew Marvell
TO HIS COY MISTRESS

Had we but world enough, and time,
This coyness, Lady, were no crime
We would sit down and think which way
To walk and pass our long love's day.
Thou by the Indian Ganges' side
Should'st rubies find: I by the tide
Of Humber would complain. I would
Love you ten years before the Flood,
And you should, if you please, refuse
Till the conversion of the Jews.
My vegetable love should grow
Vaster than empires, and more slow.
An hundred years should go to praise
Thine eyes and on thy forehead gaze;
Two hundred to adore each breast,
But thirty thousand to the rest.
An age at least to every part,
And the last age should show your heart.
For, Lady, you deserve this state,
Nor would I love at lower rate.
　　But at my back I always hear
Time's wingèd chariot hurrying near;
And yonder all before us lie
Deserts of vast eternity.
Thy beauty shall no more be found,
Nor, in thy marble vault, shall sound
My echoing song: then worms shall try
That long preserved virginity,
And your quaint honour turn to dust,
And into ashes all my lust.
The grave's a fine and private place,
But none, I think, do there embrace.
　　Now therefore, while the youthful hue
Sits on thy skin like morning dew,

And while thy willing soul transpires
At every pore with instant fires,
Now let us sport us while we may,
And now, like amorous birds of prey,
Rather at once our time devour
Than languish in his slow-chapt power.
Let us roll all our strength and all
Our sweetness up into one ball,
And tear our pleasures with rough strife
Through the iron gates of life:
Thus, though we cannot make our sun
Stand still, yet we will make him run.

John Masefield
CARGOES

Quinquireme of Nineveh from distant Ophir
Rowing home to haven in sunny Palestine,
With a cargo of ivory,
And apes and peacocks,
Sandalwood, cedarwood, and sweet white wine.

Stately Spanish galleon coming from the Isthmus,
Dipping through the Tropics by the palm-green shores,
With a cargo of diamonds,
Emeralds, amethysts,
Topazes, and cinnamon, and gold moidores.

Dirty British coaster with a salt-caked smoke stack
Butting through the Channel in the mad March days,
With a cargo of Tyne coal,
Road-rail, pig-lead,
Firewood, iron-ware, and cheap tin trays.

Edna St. Vincent Millay
TIME DOES NOT BRING RELIEF

Time does not bring relief; you all have lied
Who told me time would ease me of my pain!
I miss him in the weeping of the rain;
I want him at the shrinking of the tide;
The old snows melt from every mountain-side,
And last year's leaves are smoke in every lane;
But last year's bitter loving must remain
Heaped on my heart, and my old thoughts abide.
There are a hundred places where I fear
To go – so with his memory they brim.
And entering with relief some quiet place
Where never fell his foot or shone his face
I say, 'There is no memory of him here!'
And so stand stricken, so remembering him.

Alice Duer Miller
From THE WHITE CLIFFS

I have loved England, dearly and deeply,
Since that first morning, shining and pure,
The white cliffs of Dover I saw rising steeply
Out of the sea that once made her secure.

I had no thought then of husband or lover,
I was a traveller, the guest of a week;
Yet when they pointed 'the white cliffs of Dover',
Startled I found there were tears on my cheek.

I have loved England, and still as a stranger,
Here is my home and I still am alone.
Now in her hour of trial and danger,
Only the English are really her own.

*   *   *   *

When the sun shines on England, it atones
For low-hung leaden skies, and rain and dim
Moist fogs that paint the verdure on her stones
And fill her gentle rivers to the brim.

When the sun shines on England, shafts of light
Fall on far towers and hills and dark old trees,
And hedge-bound meadows of a green as bright –
As bright as is the blue of tropic seas.

When the sun shines, it is as if the face
Of some proud man relaxed his haughty stare,
And smiled upon us with a sudden grace,
Flattering because its coming is so rare.

And were they not English, our forefathers, never more
English than when they shook the dust of her sod
From their feet for ever, angrily seeking a shore
Where in his own way a man might worship his God.
Never more English than when they dared to be
Rebels against her – that stern intractable sense
Of that which no man can stomach and still be free,
Writing: 'When in the course of human events . . .'
Writing it out so all the world could see
Whence come the powers of all just governments.
The tree of Liberty grew and changed and spread,
But the seed was English.

        I am American bred,
I have seen much to hate here – much to forgive,
But in a world where England is finished and dead,
I do not wish to live.

Harold Monro
MILK FOR THE CAT

When the tea is brought at five o'clock,
And all the neat curtains are drawn with care,
The little black cat with bright green eyes
Is suddenly purring there.

At first she pretends, having nothing to do,
She has come in merely to blink by the grate,
But, though tea may be late or the milk may be sour,
She is never late.

And presently her agate eyes
Take a soft large milky haze,
And her independent casual glance
Becomes a stiff hard gaze.

Then she stamps her claws or lifts her ears,
Or twists her tail and begins to stir,
Till suddenly all her lithe body becomes
One breathing trembling purr.

The children eat and wriggle and laugh;
The two old ladies stroke their silk:
But the cat is grown small and thin with desire,
Transformed to a creeping lust for milk.

The white saucer like some full moon descends
At last from the clouds of the table above;
She sighs and dreams and thrills and glows,
Transfigured with love.

She nestles over the shining rim,
Buries her chin in the creamy sea;
Her tail hangs loose; each drowsy paw
Is doubled under each bending knee.

A long dim ecstasy holds her life;
Her world is an infinite shapeless white,
Till her tongue has curled the last holy drop,
Then she sinks back into the night,

Draws and dips her body to heap
Her sleepy nerves in the great arm-chair,
Lies defeated and buried deep
Three or four hours unconscious there.

William Morris
THE HAYSTACK IN THE FLOODS

Had she come all the way for this,
To part at last without a kiss?
Yea, had she borne the dirt and rain
That her own eyes might see him slain
Beside the haystack in the floods?

Along the dripping leafless woods,
The stirrup touching either shoe,
She rode astride as troopers do;
With kirtle kilted to her knee,
To which the mud splashed wretchedly;
And the wet dripped from every tree
Upon her head and heavy hair,
And on her eyelids broad and fair;
The tears and rain ran down her face.
By fits and starts they rode apace,
And very often was his place
Far off from her; he had to ride
Ahead, to see what might betide
When the roads crossed; and sometimes, when
There rose a murmuring from his men,
Had to turn back with promises;

Ah me! she had but little ease;
And often for pure doubt and dread
She sobbed, made giddy in the head
By the swift riding; while, for cold,
Her slender fingers scarce could hold
The wet reins; yea, and scarcely, too,
She felt the foot within her shoe
Against the stirrup: all for this,
To part at last without a kiss
Beside the haystack in the floods.

For when they neared that old soaked hay,
They saw across the only way
That Judas, Godmar, and the three
Red running lions dismally
Grinned from his pennon, under which
In one straight line along the ditch,
They counted thirty heads.

                    So then,
While Robert turned round to his men,
She saw at once the wretched end,
And, stooping down, tried hard to rend
Her coif the wrong way from her head,
And hid her eyes; while Robert said:
'Nay, love, 'tis scarcely two to one,
At Poictiers where we made them run
So fast — why, sweet my love, good cheer.
The Gascon frontier is so near,
Nought after this.'

      But, 'O,' she said,
'My God! my God! I have to tread
The long way back without you; then
The court at Paris; those six men;
The gratings of the Chatelet;
The swift Seine on some rainy day

Like this, and people standing by,
And laughing, while my weak hands try
To recollect how strong men swim.
All this, or else a life with him,
For which I should be damned at last,
Would God that this next hour were past!'

He answered not, but cried his cry,
'St George for Marny!' cheerily;
And laid his hand upon her rein.
Alas! no man of all his train
Gave back that cheery cry again;
And, while for rage his thumb beat fast
Upon his sword-hilts, some one cast
About his neck a kerchief long,
And bound him.

                Then they went along
To Godmar; who said: 'Now, Jehane,
Your lover's life is on the wane
So fast, that, if this very hour
You yield not as my paramour,
He will not see the rain leave off-
Nay, keep your tongue from gibe and scoff,
Sir Robert, or I slay you now.'

She laid her hand upon her brow,
Then gazed upon the palm, as though
She thought her forehead bled, and - 'No.'
She said, and turned her head away,
As there were nothing else to say,
And everything were settled: red
Grew Godmar's face from chin to head:
'Jehane, on yonder hill there stands
My castle, guarding well my lands:
What hinders me from taking you,
And doing that I list to do

To your fair wilful body, while
Your knight lies dead?

             A wicked smile
Wrinkled her face, her lips grew thin,
A long way out she thrust her chin:
'You know that I should strangle you
While you were sleeping; or bite through
Your throat, by God's help – ah!' she said,
'Lord Jesus, pity your poor maid!
For in such wise they hem me in,
I cannot choose but sin and sin,
Whatever happens: yet I think
They could not make me eat or drink,
And so should I just reach my rest.'
'Nay, if you do not my behest,
O Jehane! though I love you well,'
Said Godmar, 'would I fail to tell
All that I know.' 'Foul lies,' she said.
'Eh? lies my Jehane? by God's head,
At Paris folks would deem them true!
Do you know, Jehane, they cry for you,
"Jehane the brown! Jehane the brown!
Give us Jehane to burn or drown!" –
Eh – gag me Robert! – sweet my friend,
This were indeed a piteous end
For those long fingers, and long feet,
And long neck, and smooth shoulders sweet;
An end that few men would forget
That saw it – So, an hour yet:
Consider, Jehane, which to take
Of life or death!'

           So, scarce awake,
Dismounting, did she leave that place,
And totter some yards: with her face
Turned upward to the sky she lay,

Her head on a wet heap of hay,
And fell asleep: and while she slept,
And did not dream, the minutes crept
Round to the twelve again; but she,
Being waked at last, sighed quietly,
And strangely childlike came, and said:
'I will not.' Straightway Godmar's head,
As though it hung on strong wires, turned
Most sharply round, and his face burned.

For Robert – both his eyes were dry,
He could not weep, but gloomily
He seemed to watch the rain; yea, too,
His lips were firm; he tried once more
To touch her lips; she reached out, sore
And vain desire so tortured them,
The poor grey lips, and now the hem
Of his sleeve brushed them.

                              With a start
Up Godmar rose, thrust them apart;
From Robert's throat he loosed the bands
Of silk and mail; the empty hands
Held out, she stood and gazed, and saw,
The long bright blade without a flaw
Glide out from Godmar's sheath, his hand
In Robert's hair; she saw him bend
Back Robert's head; she saw him send
The thin steel down; the blow told well,
Right backward the knight Robert fell,
And moaned as dogs do, being half dead,
Unwitting, as I deem: so then
Godmar turned grinning to his men,
Who ran, some five or six, and beat
His head to pieces at their feet.

Then Godmar turned again and said:
'So, Jehane, the first fitte is read!
Take note, my lady, that your way
Lies backward to the Chatelet!'
She shook her head and gazed awhile,
At her cold hands with a rueful smile,
As though this thing had made her mad.

This was the parting that they had
Beside the haystack in the floods.

Edwin Muir
THE HORSES

Barely a twelvemonth after
The seven days war that put the world to sleep,
Late in the evening the strange horses came.
By then we had made our covenant with silence,
But in the first few days it was so still
We listened to our breathing and were afraid.
On the second day
The radios failed; we turned the knobs; no answer.
On the third day a warship passed us, heading north,
Dead bodies piled on the deck. On the sixth day
A plane plunged over us into the sea. Thereafter
Nothing. The radios dumb;
And still they stand in corners of our kitchens,
And stand, perhaps, turned on, in a million rooms
All over the world. But now if they should speak,
If on a sudden they should speak again,
If on the stroke of noon a voice should speak,
We would not listen, we would not let it bring
That old bad world that swallowed its children quick
At one great gulp. We would not have it again.
Sometimes we think of the nations lying asleep,

Curled blindly in impenetrable sorrow,
And then the thought confounds us with its strangeness.
The tractors lie about our fields; at evening
They look like dank sea-monsters couched and waiting.
We leave them where they are and let them rust:
'They'll moulder away and be like other loam.'
We make our oxen drag our rusty ploughs,
Long laid aside. We have gone back
Far past our fathers' land.

          And then, that evening
Late in the summer the strange horses came.
We heard a distant tapping on the road,
A deepening drumming; it stopped, went on again
And at the corner changed to hollow thunder.
We saw the heads
Like a wild wave charging and were afraid.
We had sold our horses in our fathers' time
To buy new tractors. Now they were strange to us
As fabulous steeds set on an ancient shield
Or illustrations in a book of knights.
We did not dare go near them. Yet they waited,
Stubborn and shy, as if they had been sent
By an old command to find our whereabouts
And that long-lost archaic companionship.
In the first moment we had never a thought
That they were creatures to be owned and used.
Among them were some half-a-dozen colts
Dropped in some wilderness of the broken world,
Yet new as if they had come from their own Eden.
Since then they have pulled our ploughs and borne our
    loads
But that free servitude still can pierce our hearts.
Our life is changed; their coming our beginning.

Alfred Noyes
THE OLD GREY SQUIRREL

A great while ago, there was a schoolboy.
   He lived in a cottage by the sea;
And the very first thing he could remember
   Was the rigging of the schooners by the quay.

He could watch them when he woke, from his window,
   With the tall cranes hoisting out the freight;
And he used to think of shipping as a sea-cook,
   And sailing to the Golden Gate.

For he used to buy the yellow penny dreadfuls,
   And read them where he fished for conger-eels,
And listened to the lapping of the water,
   The green and oily water round the keels.

There were trawlers with their shark-mouth
   And red nets hanging out to dry,
And the skate the skipper kept because
   And landsmen never knew the fish

There were brigantines with timb
   Oozing with the syrups of th
There were rusty dusty schoo
   And ships of the Blue Cr

And to tumble down a evening,
   Was better than th
For the smell of 'en
   And the feel of

And, before
   The very
Was the s
   By th

He is perched upon a high stool in London.
　　The Golden Gate is very far away.
They caught him, and they caged him, like a squirrel.
　　He is totting up accounts, and going grey.

He will never, never, never sail to 'Frisco
　　But the very last thing that he will see
Will be sailor-men a-dancing in the sunrise
　　By the capstan that stood upon the quay . . .

To the tune of an old concertina,
　　By the capstan that stood upon the quay.

Arthur William Edgar O'Shaughnessy
ODE (WE ARE THE MUSIC MAKERS)

We are the music-makers,
　　And we are the dreamers of dreams,
Wandering by lone sea-breakers,
　　And sitting by desolate streams;
-losers and world forsakers,
　　om the pale moon gleams:
　　he movers and shakers
　　for ever, it seems.

　　less ditties
　　reat cities.

We, in the ages lying
   In the buried past of the earth,
Built Nineveh with our sighing,
   And Babel itself with our mirth;
And o'erthrew them with prophesying
   To the old of the new world's worth;
For each age is a dream that is dying,
   Or one that is coming to birth.

Herbert Edward Palmer
THE WOODWORKER'S BALLAD

All that is moulded of iron
Has lent to destruction and blood;
But the things that are honoured of Zion
Are most of them made from wood.

Stone can be chiselled to Beauty,
And iron shines bright for Defence;
But when Mother Earth pondered her duty
She brought forth the forest, from whence

Come tables, and chairs, and crosses,
Little things that a hot fire warps,
Old ships that the blue wave tosses,
And fiddles for music, and harps;

Oak boards where the carved ferns mingle,
Monks' shrines in the wilderness,
Snug little huts in the dingle,
All things that the sad poets bless.

King Arthur had a wood table;
And Our Lord blessed wood; for, you see,
He was born in a wooden stable,
And He died on a wooden tree;

And He sailed in a wooden vessel
On the waters of Galilee,
And He worked at a wooden trestle,
At His wonderful carpentry.

Oh, all that is moulded of iron
Has lent to destruction and blood;
But the things that are honoured of Zion
Are most of them made from wood.

Dorothy Parker
ONE PERFECT ROSE

A single flow'r he sent me, since we met.
    All tenderly his messenger he chose;
Deep-hearted, pure, with scented dew still wet –
    One perfect rose.

I knew the language of the floweret;
    'My fragile leaves,' it said, 'his heart enclose.'
Love long has taken for his amulet
    One perfect rose.   ———

Why is it no one ever sent me yet
    One perfect limousine, do you suppose?
Ah no, it's always just my luck to get
    One perfect rose.

Ruth Pitter
THE RUDE POTATO

By jobbing Jimmy this was found
Last autumn as he delved the ground
To get the late potatoes up
And save the nice clean heavy crop.
He saw it was irregular,
As these large tubers often are;
A second glance convinced old Jas.
Just how irregular it was.
Comic potatoes do occur,
But in the life of Jimmy Burr
Who's handled many score of tons
And spotted all the funny ones,
This was the rudest he had met.
Its shamelessness was quite complete,
Warming the honest gardener's heart
By asking no least touch of art,
Which nearly all such gems require
To make them apt to our desire.

No nugget of the purest ore
Could have delighted Jimmy more.
A slow, profound, and spreading grin
Proclaimed the gratitude within:
Then on a handy frame he laid
The treasure, and resumed the spade –
Or stay – no doubt resumed the fork,
Which is more usual for such work.

Emerging from the kitchen door
Comes Mitzi (from the Danube shore)
For parsley, or some subtler weed
Such as these foreign artists need.
She spots the tuber on the frame,

And stops to scrutinise the same.
Then O what peals of peasant mirth
Explode above our chilly earth!
She shrieks, bends double, beats her thighs;
She clasps her sides; then wipes her eyes
To get another look, and then
She has gone off in fits again.
And all the day, when here and there
She has a little time to spare,
She comes; and one refreshing peep
Such dews of joy can make her weep,
That all her sorrows seem to fade,
And glee transforms the exiled maid.
Hark! as she dishes up, she sings
What sound like wild Danubian things;
And later, at the fall of night,
'Roll Out the Barrel' *almost* right.
Fain would she keep the glorious thing,
That makes a lonely exile sing;
But Jimmy takes it, when he goes
To taste the nectar at the 'Rose
And Crown', when all our worthies are
Gathered at evening in the bar.

The slighter spirits yell with glee
The freakish masterpiece to see,
But stately Drake, the landlord, winks
At Jimmy Burr above the drinks,
And gravely hangs the wonder up
For all to see who take a cup,
Then gives old Jim two ten-bob notes,
Which go to slake the assembled throats.
'That's Nature!' says imposing Drake:
'Now, gentlemen, what will you take?'

O Science! can you make us mirth
Like this dull apple of the earth?
And what in art can do us good
Like this, so nourishing, so lewd?
Only by life such joy is lent,
Wild, bracing, and inconsequent.

Alexander Pope
ODE ON SOLITUDE

Happy the man, whose wish and care
  A few paternal acres bound,
Content to breathe his native air
          In his own ground.

Whose herds with milk, whose fields with bread,
  Whose flocks supply him with attire,
Whose trees in summer yield him shade,
          In winter fire.

Blest, who can unconcern'dly find
  Hours, days, and years slide soft away,
In health of body, peace of mind,
          Quiet by day.

Sound sleep by night; study and ease,
  Together mixt; sweet recreation:
And innocence, which most does please
          With meditation.

Thus let me live, unseen, unknown,
  Thus unlamented let me die,
Steal from the world, and not a stone
          Tell where I lie.

Adelaide Anne Procter
ONE BY ONE

One by one the sands are flowing,
　One by one the moments fall;
Some are coming, some are going;
　Do not strive to grasp them all.

One by one thy duties wait thee,
　Let thy whole strength go to each,
Let no future dreams elate thee,
　Learn thou first what these can teach.

One by one (bright gifts from Heaven)
　Joys are sent thee here below;
Take them readily when given,
　Ready too to let them go.

One by one griefs shall meet thee,
　Do not fear an armèd band;
One will fade as others greet thee;
　Shadows passing through the land.

Do not look at life's long sorrow;
　See how small each moment's pain;
God will help thee for to-morrow,
　So each day begin again.

Every hour that fleets so slowly
　Has its task to do or bear;
Luminous the crown, and holy,
　When each gem is set with care.

Do not linger with regretting,
　Or for passing hours despond;
Nor, the daily toil forgetting,
　Look too eagerly beyond.

Hours are golden links, God's token
  Reaching Heaven; but one by one
Take them, lest the chain be broken
  Ere the pilgrimage be done.

W.B. Rands
THE PEDLAR'S CARAVAN

I wish I lived in a caravan,
With a horse to drive, like a pedlar-man!
Where he comes from nobody knows,
Nor where he goes to, but on he goes.

His caravan has windows two,
With a chimney of tin that the smoke comes through,
He has a wife, and a baby brown,
And they go riding from town to town.

Chairs to mend and delf to sell –
He clashes the basins like a bell.
Tea-trays, baskets, ranged in order,
Plates, with the alphabet round the border.

The roads are brown, and the sea is green,
But his house is just like a bathing machine.
The world is round, but he can ride,
Rumble, and splash to the other side.

With the pedlar-man I should like to roam,
And write a book when I come home.
All the people would read my book,
Just like the Travels of Captain Cook.

Henry Reed
LESSONS OF THE WAR (TO ALAN MICHELL)

Vixi duellis nuper idoneus
Et militavi non sine gloria

1. NAMING OF PARTS.

To-day we have naming of parts. Yesterday,
We had daily cleaning. And to-morrow morning,
We shall have what to do after firing. But to-day,
To-day we have naming of parts. Japonica
Glistens like coral in all of the neighbouring gardens,
    And to-day we have naming of parts.

This is the lower sling swivel. And this
Is the upper sling swivel, whose use you will see,
When you are given your slings. And this is the piling swivel,
Which in your case you have not got. The branches
Hold in the gardens their silent, eloquent gestures,
    Which in our case we have not got.

This is the safety-catch, which is always released
With an easy flick of the thumb. And please do not let me
See anyone using his finger. You can do it quite easy
If you have any strength in your thumb. The blossoms
Are fragile and motionless, never letting anyone see
    Any of them using their finger.

And this you can see is the bolt. The purpose of this
Is to open the breech, as you see. We can slide it
Rapidly backwards and forwards: we call this
Easing the spring. And rapidly backwards and forwards
The early bees are assaulting and fumbling the flowers:
    They call it easing the Spring.

They call it easing the Spring; it is perfectly easy
If you have any strength in your thumb: like the bolt,
And the breech, and the cocking-piece, and the point of
    balance,
Which in our case we have not got; and the almond blossom
Silent in all of the gardens and the bees going backwards
    and forwards,
      For to-day we have naming of parts.

Christina Rossetti
UPHILL

Does the road wind uphill all the way?
   Yes, to the very end.
Will the day's journey take the whole long day?
   From morn to night, my friend.

But is there for the night a resting-place?
   A roof for when the slow, dark hours begin.
May not the darkness hide it from my face?
   You cannot miss that inn.

Shall I meet other wayfarers at night?
   Those who have gone before.
Then must I knock, or call when just in sight?
   They will not keep you waiting at that door.

Shall I find comfort, travel-sore and weak?
   Of labour you shall find the sum.
Will there be beds for me and all who seek?
   Yea, beds for all who come.

Alan Seeger
I HAVE A RENDEZVOUS WITH DEATH

I have a rendezvous with Death
At some disputed barricade,
When Spring comes back with rustling shade
And apple blossoms fill the air –
I have a rendezvous with Death
When Spring brings back blue days and fair.

It may be he shall take my hand,
And lead me into his dark land,
And close my eyes and quench my breath –
It may be I shall pass him still.
I have a rendezvous with Death
On some scarred slope of battered hill,
When Spring comes round again this year
And the first meadow flowers appear.

God knows 'twere better to be deep
Pillowed in silk and scented down,
Where Love throbs out in blissful sleep,
Pulse nigh to pulse, and breath to breath,
Where hushed awakenings are dear . . . .
But I've a rendezvous with Death
At midnight in some flaming town,
When Spring trips north again this year;
And I to my pledged word am true,
I shall not fail that rendezvous.

Edward Shanks
THE OTHER LITTLE BOATS: JULY 1588

A pause came in the fighting and England held her breath
For the battle was not ended and the ending might be death.
Then out they came, the little boats, from all the Channel
    shore
Free men were these who set the sails and laboured at the
    oars.
From Itchenor and Shoreham, from Deal and Winchelsea,
They put out into the Channel to keep their country free.
Not of Dunkirk this story, but of boatmen long ago,
When our Queen was Gloriana and King Philip was our foe
And galleons rode the Narrow Sea, and Effingham and Drake
Were out of shot and powder, with all England still at stake.
They got the shot and powder, they charged their guns
    again,
The guns that guarded England from the galleons of Spain,
And the men who helped them to do it, helped them still to
    hold the sea
Men from Itchenor and Shoreham, men from Deal and
    Winchelsea,
Looked out happily from Heaven and cheered to see the
    work
Of their grandsons' grandsons' grandsons on the beaches of
    Dunkirk.

Percy Bysshe Shelley
OZYMANDIAS

I met a traveller from an antique land
Who said: 'Two vast and trunkless legs of stone
Stand in the desert. Near them, on the sand
Half sunk, a shattered visage lies, whose frown,

And wrinkled lip, and sneer of cold command,
Tell that its sculptor well those passions read
Which yet survive, stamped on these lifeless things,
The hand that mocked them, and the heart that fed;
And on the pedestal these words appear:
"My name is Ozymandias, king of kings:
Look on my works, ye Mighty, and despair!"
Nothing beside remains. Round the decay
Of that colossal wreck, boundless and bare
The lone and level sands stretch far away.'

Frank Sidgwick
A CHRISTMAS LEGEND

Abroad on a winter's night there ran
Under the starlight, leaping the rills
Swollen with snow-drip from the hills,
  Goat-legged, goat-bearded Pan.

He loved to run on the crisp white floor,
Where black hill-torrents chiselled grooves,
And he loved to print his clean-cut hooves,
  Where none had trod before.

And now he slacked and came to a stand
Beside a river too broad to leap;
And as he panted he heard a sheep
  That bleated near at hand.

'Bell-wether, bell-wether, what do you say?
Peace, and huddle your ewes from cold!'
'Master, but ere we went to fold
  Our herdsman hastened away:

'Over the hill came other twain
And pointed away to Bethlehem,
And spake with him, and he followed them,
   And has not come again.

'He dropped his pipe of the river-reed;
He left his scrip in his haste to go;
And all our grazing is under snow,
   So that we cannot feed.'

'Left his sheep on a winter's night?' –
Pan folded them with an angry frown.
'Bell-wether, bell-wether, I'll go down
   Where the star shines bright.'

Down by the hamlet he met the man.
'Shepherd, no shepherd, thy flock is lorn!'
'Master, no master, a child is born
   Royal, greater than Pan.

'Lo, I have seen; I go to my sheep;
Follow my footsteps through the snow,
But warily, warily see thou go,
   For child and mother sleep.'

Into the stable-yard Pan crept,
And there in a manger a baby lay
Beside his mother upon the hay,
   And mother and baby slept.

Pan bent over the sleeping child,
Gazed on him, panting after his run:
And while he wondered, the little one
   Opened his eyes and smiled;

Smiled, and after a little space
Struggled an arm from the swaddling-band
And raising a tiny dimpled hand,
   Patted the bearded face.

Something snapped in the breast of Pan;
His heart, his throat, his eyes were sore,
And he wished to weep as never before
   Since the world began.

And out he went to the silly sheep,
To the fox on the hill, the fish in the sea,
The horse in the stall, the bird in the tree,
   Asking them how to weep.

They could not teach – they did not know;
The law stands writ for the beast that's dumb
That a limb may ache and a heart be numb,
   But never a tear can flow.

So bear you kindly to-day, O Man
To all that is dumb and all that is wild,
For the sake of the Christmas Babe who smiled
   In the eyes of great god Pan.

Jon Silkin
DEATH OF A SON

(Who died in a mental Hospital aged one)

   Something has ceased to come along with me.
Something like a person: something very like one.
    And there was no nobility in it
      Or anything like that.

Something was there like a one year
Old house, dumb as stone. While the near buildings
   Sang like birds and laughed
     Understanding the pact

They were to have with silence. But he
Neither sang nor laughed. He did not bless silence
   Like bread, with words.
     He did not forsake silence.

But rather, like a house in mourning
Kept the eye turned in to watch the silence while
   The other houses like birds
     Sang around him.

And the breathing silence neither
Moved nor was still.

I have seen stones: I have seen brick
But this house was made up of neither bricks nor stone
   But a house of flesh and blood
     With flesh of stone

And bricks for blood. A house
Of stones and blood in breathing silence with the other
   Birds singing crazy on its chimneys.
     But this was silence,

There was something else, this was
Hearing and speaking though he was a house drawn
   Into silence, this was
     Something religious in his silence,

Something shining in his quiet,
This was different, this was altogether something else:
 Though he never spoke, this
  Was something to do with death.

 And then slowly the eye stopped looking
Inward. The silence rose and became still.
The look turned to the outer place and stopped,
 With the birds still shrilling around him.
  And as if he could speak

He turned over on his side with his one year
Red as a wound
He turned over as if he could be sorry for this
And out of his eyes two great tears rolled, like stones, and
 he died.

C. Marjorie Smith
CONSUMER COMPLAINT

When I was young – say, three or four –
I was not put to ride, astride,
A trolley round a Super Store.
Nor wheeled between the loaded shelves
From which the shoppers helped themselves,
Nor did I dare to raise my voice
Demanding goodies of my choice.

No! I was lifted on a stool
My dangling, gaitered legs to cool,
Bidden sit quietly – 'Not a word!
Nice children should be seen, not heard!'

Hatted and veiled, and also seated,
My Mother was with deference treated.
Our Grocer – (apron, bow-tie, wax moustache)
Was all attention to her pleasure,
Gave his opinion of the weather,
Touched civilly on this and that
While pouring sugar on to flat
Thick squares of paper – fold and twist,
Tuck in the corners – who could wish
A neater package? Then to hold the thing
He made a finger-loop of string!
(No smart machine to snip and snap
No sealing tape – or plastic wrap!)

From creamy kegs this clever chap
Sliced off two pounds of butter! Slapped
And shaped it with a wooden pat.
Intricate scrolls of red and gold
Patterned tall cannisters and told
What brands of tea were stored within.

Biscuits from an enormous tin
Were weighed out, loose, in paper bags –
(Oh how frustrated, now, I drag
At layers of cellophane that snag
My finger nails!) . . .
, . . Straw-boated butcher in his shop
Of hanging carcases, would slice the chop
That took one's fancy . . .
                    Oh! for hours
One could compare the Now and Then! . . .
Murdered by customer-protection men
Those gracious days will not return again.

John Smith
SOMEWHERE AROUND CHRISTMAS

Always, or nearly always, on old apple trees,
Somewhere around Christmas, if you look up through the
    forest,
You will see, fat as a bullfinch, stuck on a high branch,
One lingering, bald, self-sufficient, hard, blunt fruit.

There will be no leaves, you can be sure of that;
The twigs will be tar black, and the white sky
Will be grabbed among the branches like thumbed glass
In broken triangles just saved from crashing to the ground.

Further up, dribbles of rain will run down
Like spilt colourless varnish on a canvas. The old tins,
Tyres, cardboard boxes, debris of back gardens,
Will lie around, bleak, with mould and rust creeping over
    them.

Blow on your fingers. Wipe your feet on the mat by the back
    door.
You will never see that apple fall. Look at the cat,
Her whiskers twitch as she sleeps by the kitchen fire;
In her backyard-prowling dream she thinks it's a bird.

Robert Southey
THE WELL OF ST. KEYNE

A well there is in the west country,
    And a clearer one never was seen;
There is not a wife in the west country
    But has heard of the Well of St. Keyne.

An oak and an elm-tree stand beside,
   And behind doth an ash-tree grow,
And a willow from the bank above
   Droops to the water below.

A traveller came to the well of St. Keyne;
   Joyfully he drew nigh,
For from cock-crow he had been travelling,
   And there was not a cloud in the sky.

He drank of the water so cool and clear,
   For thirsty and hot was he,
And he sat down upon the bank
   Under the willow-tree.

There came a man from the house hard by
   At the Well to fill his pail;
On the Well-side he rested it,
   And he bade the Stranger hail.

'Now art thou a bachelor, Stranger?' quoth he,
   'For an if thou hast a wife,
The happiest draught thou hast drank this day
   That ever thou didst in thy life.

'Or has thy good woman, if one thou hast,
   Ever here in Cornwall been?
For an if she have, I'll venture my life
   She has drank of the Well of St. Keyne.'

'I have left a good woman who never was here,'
   The Stranger he made reply,
'But that my draught should be the better for that,
   I pray you answer me why?'

'St. Keyne,' quoth the Cornish-man, 'many a time
    Drank of this crystal Well,
And before the Angel summon'd her,
    She laid on the water a spell.

'If the Husband of this gifted Well
    Shall drink before his Wife,
A happy man thenceforth is he,
    For he shall be Master for life.

'But if the Wife should drink of it first
    God help the Husband then!'
The Stranger stoopt to the Well of St. Keyne,
    And drank of the water again.

'You drank of the Well I warrant betimes?'
    He to the Cornish-man said:
But the Cornish-man smiled as the Stranger spake,
    And sheepishly shook his head.

I hasten'd as soon as the wedding was done,
    And left my Wife in the porch;
But i' faith she had been wiser than me,
    For she took a bottle to Church.'

William Robert Spencer
BETH GELERT

The spearman heard the bugle sound,
    And cheerily smiled the morn;
And many a brach, and many a hound,
    Attend Llewellyn's horn:

And still he blew a louder blast,
   And gave a louder cheer:
'Come, Gelert! why art thou the last
   Llewellyn's horn to hear!

'Oh! where does faithful Gelert roam?
   The flower of all his race!
So true, so brave: a lamb at home,
   A lion in the chase!'

In sooth he was a peerless hound,
   The gift of royal John;
But now no Gelert could be found,
   And all the chase rode on.

And now, as over rocks and dells
   The gallant chidings rise,
All Snowdon's craggy chaos yells
   With many mingled cries.

That day Llewellyn little loved
   The chase of hart or hare!
And small and scant the booty proved,
   For Gelert was not there.

Unpleased, Llewellyn homeward hied,
   When near the portal-seat,
His truant Gelert he espied,
   Bounding his lord to greet.

But when he gained the castle door,
   Aghast the chieftain stood;
The hound was smeared with gouts of gore,
   His lips and fangs ran blood!

Llewellyn gazed with wild surprise,
   Unused such looks to meet:
His favourite checked his joyful guise,
   And crouch'd and lick'd his feet.

Onward in haste Llewellyn pass'd –
   And on went Gelert too –
And still, where'er his eyes were cast,
   Fresh blood-gouts shocked his view.

O'erturned his infant's bed, he found
   The blood-stained covert rent;
And all around, the walls and ground
   With recent blood besprent.

He call'd the child – no voice replied;
   He search'd – with terror wild;
Blood! blood! he found on every side,
   But nowhere found his child!

'Hell-hound! by thee my child's devoured!'
   The frantic father cried;
And, to the hilt, his vengeful sword
   He plunged in Gelert's side!

His suppliant, as to earth he fell,
   No pity could impart:
But still his Gelert's dying yell
   Pass'd heavy o'er his heart.

Arous'd by Gelert's dying yell
   Some slumberer waken'd nigh:
What words the parent's joy can tell,
   To hear his infant cry!

Conceal'd beneath a mangled heap,
   His hurried search had miss'd,
All glowing from his rosy sleep,
   His cherub-boy he kissed!

Nor scratch had he, nor harm,nor dread –
   But, the same couch beneath,
Lay a great wolf, all torn and dead –
   Tremendous still in death!

Ah! what was then Llewellyn's pain!
   For now the truth was clear:
The gallant hound the wolf had slain,
   To save Llewellyn's heir.

Vain, vain was all Llewellyn's woe:
   'Best of thy kind, adieu!
The frantic deed which laid thee low
   This heart shall ever rue!'

And now a gallant tomb they raise,
   With costly sculpture deck'd;
And marbles, storied with his praise,
   Poor Gelert's bones protect.

Here never could the spearman pass
   Or forester unmoved!
Here oft the tear-besprinkled grass
   Llewellyn's sorrow proved.

And here he hung his horn and spear;
   And oft, as evening fell,
In fancy's piercing sounds would hear
   Poor Gelert's dying yell.

And till great Snowden's rocks grow old,
   And cease the storm to brave,
The consecrated spot shall hold
   The name of 'Gelert's Grave.'

Robert Louis Stevenson
THE HOUSE BEAUTIFUL

A naked house, a naked moor,
A shivering pool before the door,
A garden bare of flowers and fruit
And poplars at the garden foot:
Such is the place that I live in,
Bleak without and bare within.

Yet shall your ragged moor receive
The incomparable pomp of eve,
And the cold glories of the dawn
Behind your shivering trees be drawn;
And when the wind from place to place
Doth the unmoored cloud-galleons chase,
Your garden gloom and gleam again,
With leaping sun, with glancing rain.
Here shall the wizard moon ascend
The heavens, in the crimson end
Of day's declining splendour; here
The army of the stars appear.
The neighbour hollows dry or wet,
Spring shall with tender flowers beset;
And oft the morning muser see
Larks rising from the broomy lea,
And every fairy wheel and thread
Of cobweb dew-bediamonded.
When daisies go, shall winter time
Silver the simple grass with rime;

Autumnal frosts enchant the pool
And make the cart-ruts beautiful;
And when snow-bright the moor expands,
How shall your children clap their hands!
To make this earth our heritage,
A cheerful and a changeful page,
God's bright and intricate device
Of days and seasons doth suffice.

Jan Struther
THE CUL DE SAC

Whose love's a broad highway
That stretches boldly on
Before them all the day,
White and smooth in the sun –
These, if they will, may run.
For them there is no need
To curb the hot-foot speed
Of their delight, which draws them
On over dale and hill
And from each summit shows them
A landscape lovelier still.
But whose love's no more
than a blind alley –
A cul de sac
Which can have no other end
than turning back
Or beating with bare hands
At a wall without a door –
These must go slowly.
These at a measured pace
Must walk,
And linger in one place
Often, to gaze and talk;

Even retrace
A yard or two, perhaps,
Their careful steps,
And take them over again.
Their eyes they must restrain
From seeking the far sky
And bend them to enjoy
The small delights which grow beneath their feet:
Veined, shining, curious pebbles
They must admire, and stoop
To finger the small cresses,
Stonecrops and cushioned mosses
That creep
Between the untrodden cobbles
Of that deserted street.

Gently if they are wise,
From stage to stage progresses
The grave, time-honoured dance of their caresses.
Impetuous hands must bide
Their hour, till hungry eyes
Be satisfied;
And from a finger's touch
They must distil as much
Sweetness and ravishment
As freer lovers find
In bodies intertwined.
They must eke out each kiss
With its own memory
And long foretasting of the next one's bliss:
For kisses treated so
Shall be less swift to grow
(Strange alchemy!) from butterfly to bee.

By such fond strategy,
Such passionate artifice,
They may a long while cheat
Themselves into content,
And not too deeply care
That fate across the threshold of their street
Has scrawled 'No Thoroughfare'.

G. A. Studdert-Kennedy
INDIFFERENCE

When Jesus came to Golgotha they hanged Him on a tree,
They drave great nails through hands and feet, and made a
    Calvary;
They crowned Him with a crown of thorns, red were His
    wounds and deep,
For those were crude and cruel days, the human flesh was
    cheap.

When Jesus came to Birmingham, they simply passed Him
    by,
They never hurt a hair of Him, they only let Him die;
For men had grown more tender, and they would not give
    Him pain,
They only just passed down the street, and left Him in the
    rain.

Still Jesus cried, 'Forgive them, for they know not what they
    do,'
And still it rained the winter rain that drenched Him through
    and through;
The crowds went home and left the streets without a soul to
    see,
And Jesus crouched against a wall and cried for Calvary.

Alfred, Lord Tennyson
From IN MEMORIAM A.H.H.

CVI

Ring out, wild bells, to the wild sky,
    The flying cloud, the frosty light:
    The year is dying in the night;
Ring out, wild bells, and let him die.

Ring out the old, ring in the new,
    Ring, happy bells, across the snow:
    The year is going, let him go;
Ring out the false, ring in the true.

Ring out the grief that saps the mind,
    For those that here we see no more;
    Ring out the feud of rich and poor,
Ring in redress to all mankind.

Ring out a slowly dying cause,
    And ancient forms of party strife;
    Ring in the nobler modes of life,
With sweeter manners, purer laws.

Ring out the want, the care, the sin,
    The faithless coldness of the times;
    Ring out, ring out thy mournful rhymes,
But ring the fuller minstrel in.

Ring out false pride in place and blood,
    The civic slander and the spite;
    Ring in the love of truth and right,
Ring in the common love of good.

Ring out old shapes of foul disease;
   Ring out the narrowing lust of gold;
   Ring out the thousand wars of old,
Ring in the thousand years of peace.

Ring in the valiant man and free,
   The larger heart, the kindlier hand;
   Ring out the darkness of the land,
Ring in the Christ that is to be.

Dylan Thomas
DO NOT GO GENTLE INTO THAT GOOD NIGHT

Do not go gentle into that good night,
Old age should burn and rave at close of day;
Rage, rage against the dying of the light.

Though wise men at their end know dark is right,
Because their words had forked no lightning they
Do not go gentle into that good night.

Good men, the last wave by, crying how bright
Their frail deeds might have danced in a green bay,
Rage, rage against the dying of the light.

Wild men who caught and sang the sun in flight,
And learn, too late, they grieved it on its way,
Do not go gentle into that good night.

Grave men, near death, who see with blinding sight
Blind eyes could blaze like meteors and be gay,
Rage, rage against the dying of the light.

And you, my father, there on the sad height,
Curse, bless, me now with your fierce tears, I pray.
Do not go gentle into that good night.
Rage, rage against the dying of the light.

Francis Thompson
THE HOUND OF HEAVEN

I fled Him, down the nights and down the days;
   I fled Him down the arches of the years;
I fled Him, down the labyrinthine ways
   Of my own mind; and in the mist of tears
I hid from Him, and under running laughter.
           Up vistaed hopes I sped;
           And shot, precipitated,
Adown Titanic glooms of chasmèd fears,
   From those strong Feet that followed, followed after.
         But with unhurrying chase,
         And unperturbed pace,
  Deliberate speed, majestic instancy
         They beat – and a Voice beat
         More instant than the Feet –
'All things betray thee, who betrayest Me.'

      I pleaded, outlaw-wise,
By many a hearted casement, curtained red,
   Trellised with intertwining charities;
(For, though I knew His love Who followèd,
     Yet was I sore adread
Lest, having Him, I must have naught beside);
But, if one little casement parted wide,
   The gust of His approach would clash it to.
Fear wist not to evade, as Love wist to pursue.
Across the margent of the world I fled,
   And troubled the gold gateways of the stars,

Smiting for shelter on their clangèd bars;
        Fretted to dulcet jars
And silvern chatter the pale ports o' the moon.
I said to dawn, Be sudden; to eve, Be soon;
   With thy young skiey blossoms heap me over
        From this tremendous Lover!
Float thy vague veil about me, lest He see!
   I tempted all His servitors, but to find
My own betrayal in their constancy,
In faith to Him their fickleness to me,
   Their traitorous trueness, and their loyal deceit.
To all swift things for swiftness did I sue;
Clung to the whistling mane of every wind.
     But whether they swept, smoothly fleet,
   The long savannahs of the blue;
        Or whether, Thunder-driven,
   They clanged his chariot 'thwart a heaven
Plashy with flying lightnings round the spurn o' their feet:
   Fear wist not to evade as Love wist to pursue.
        Still with unhurrying chase,
        And unperturbed pace,
   Deliberate speed, majestic instancy,
        Came on the following Feet,
        And a Voice above their beat –
'Naught shelters thee, who wilt not shelter Me.'

        Now of that long pursuit
        Comes on at hand the bruit;
   That Voice is round me like a bursting sea:
      'And is thy earth so marred,
      Shattered in shard on shard?
Lo, all things fly thee, for thou fliest Me!

   Strange, piteous, futile thing,
Wherefore should any set thee love apart?
Seeing none but I makes much of naught' (He said)
'And human love needs human meriting:

How hast thou merited –
Of all man's clotted clay the dingiest clot?
Alack, thou knowest not
How little worthy of any love thou art!
Whom wilt thou find to love ignoble thee
Save Me, save only Me?
All which I took from thee I did but take,
Not for thy harms,
But just that thou might'st seek it in My arms.
All which thy child's mistake
Fancies as lost, I have stored for thee at home:
Rise, clasp My hand, and come!'

Halts by me that footfall:
Is my gloom, after all,
Shade of His hand, outstretched caressingly?
'Ah, fondest, blindest, weakest,
I am He Whom thou seekest!
Thou dravest love from thee, who dravest Me.'

Chidiock Titchborne
MY PRIME OF YOUTH

(written the night before his execution)

My prime of youth is but a frost of cares;
My feast of joy is but a dish of pain;
My crop of corn is but a field of tares;
And all my good is but vain hope of gain;
My life is fled, and yet I saw no sun;
And now I live, and now my life is done.

The spring is past, and yet it hath not sprung;
The fruit is dead, and yet the leaves be green;
My youth is gone, and yet I am but young;

I saw the world, and yet I was not seen;
My thread is cut, and yet it is not spun;
And now I live, and now my life is done.

I sought my death, and found it in my womb,
I looked for life, and saw it was a shade,
I trod the earth and knew it was my tomb,
And now I die, and now I am but made:
The glass is full, and now my glass is run,
And now I live, and now my life is done.

Rowena Touquet
BILLY TWIGGER'S FANCY

They said his feet were never on the ground,
You couldn't ever hope to know his mind –
Who owns the rainbow or can kiss the wind?
He always had two minds, and sometimes three.

He liked his glass dome full of coloured birds,
Forget to knock you'd hear the whirr of wings.
Angels were dancing in his apple tree,
His bonfire's ash had warmed a phoenix egg,
His tattered shed had kept a unicorn,
Tiger or star, he wasn't quite sure which.
If you had stared, reflected in his eyes,
Submerged in that opaque you'd see the thought
As startling as a mermaid in the pond.

His girl was just the same, and when she died,
He'd lean against the barn a gilt-edged day –
He didn't speak – we knew that he still saw
Her little pointed shoe against the snow.

Mary Webb
GOING FOR THE MILK

Going for the milk –
A toddling child with skin like curds,
On a May morning in a charm of birds:

Going for the milk
With laughing, teasing lads, at seventeen,
With rosy cheeks and breast as soft as silk –
Eh! what a mort of years between!

Going for the milk
Through my Jim's garden, past the bush o' balm,
With my first baby sleeping on my arm:

It's fifty year, come Easter, since that day;
The work'us ward is cold, my eyes be dim;
Never no more I'll go the flowery way,
Fetching the milk. I drink the pauper's skim,
And mind me of those summer days, and Jim
Telling me as my breast was soft as silk –
And that first day I missed to fetch the milk.

John Greenleaf Whittier
THE PIPES AT LUCKNOW

Pipes of the misty moorlands,
    Voice of the glens and hills;
The droning of the torrents,
    The treble of the rills!
Not the braes of broom and heather,
    Nor the mountains dark with rain,
Nor maiden bower, nor border tower,
    Have heard your sweetest strain!

Dear to the Lowland reaper,
  And plaided mountaineer, –
To the cottage and the castle
  The Scottish pipes are dear –
Sweet sounds the ancient pibroch
  O'er mountain, loch, and glade;
But the sweetest of all music
  The pipes at Lucknow played.

Day by day the Indian tiger
  Louder yelled, and nearer crept;
Round and round the jungle-serpent
  Near and nearer circles swept.
'Pray for rescue, wives and mothers, –
  Pray to-day!' the soldier said;
'To-morrow, death's between us
  And the wrong and shame we dread.'

Oh, they listened, looked, and waited,
  Till their hope became despair;
And the sobs of low bewailing
  Filled the pauses of their prayer.
Then up spake a Scottish maiden,
  With her ear unto the ground:
Dinna ye hear it? – dinna ye hear it?
  The pipes o' Havelock sound!'

Hushed the wounded man his groaning;
  Hushed the wife her little ones;
Alone they heard the drum-roll
  And the roar of Sepoy guns.
But to sounds of home and childhood
  The Highland ear was true; –
As her mother's cradle-crooning
  The mountain pipes she knew.

Like the march of soundless music
   Through the vision of the seer,
More of feeling than of hearing,
   Of the heart than of the ear
She knew the droning pibroch,
   She knew the Campbell's call
'Hark! hear ye no' MacGregor's,
   The grandest o' them all!'

Oh, they listened, dumb and breathless,
   And they caught the sound at last;
Faint and far beyond the Goomtee
   Rose and fell the piper's blast!
Then a burst of wild thanksgiving
   Mingled woman's voice and man's;
'God be praised! – the march of Havelock!
   The piping of the clans!'

Louder, nearer, fierce as vengeance,
   Sharp and shrill as swords at strife,
Came the wild MacGregor's clan-call,
   Stinging all the air to life.
But when the far-off dust-cloud
   To plaided legions grew,
Full tenderly and blithesomely
   The pipes of rescue blew!

Round the silver domes of Lucknow,
   Moslem mosque and Pagan shrine,
Breathed the air to Britons dearest,
   The air of Auld Lang Syne.
O'er the cruel roll of war-drums
   Rose that sweet and homelike strain;
And the tartan clove the turban,
   As the Goomtee cleaves the plain.

Dear to the corn-land reaper
  And plaided mountaineer, –
To the cottage and the castle
  The piper's song is dear.
Sweet sounds the Gaelic pibroch
  O'er mountain, glen, and glade;
But the sweetest of all music
  The Pipes at Lucknow played!

Lorna Wood
TO A DESCENDANT

I shall not be an importunate, nagging ghost,
Sighing for unsaid prayers: or a family spectre
Advertising that someone is due to join me . . . .
Nor one who has to be exorcised by the Rector.

I shall not be the commercial type of ghost,
Pointing to boxes of gold under the floor
And I certainly don't intend to jangle chains
Or carry my head . . . (such a guesome type of chore!)

I shall not cause draughts, be noisy, spoil your 'let', –
In fact, to be brief, I shan't materialise.
But I shall be pleased if anyone ever sees me
In your face or your walk or the glance of your laughing
    eyes.

William Wordsworth
WE ARE SEVEN

– A simple Child,
That lightly draws its breath,
And feels its life in every limb,
What should it know of death?

I met a little cottage Girl:
She was eight years old, she said;
Her hair was thick with many a curl
That clustered round her head.

She had a rustic, woodland air,
And she was wildly clad:
Her eyes were fair, and very fair;
– Her beauty made me glad.

'Sisters and brothers, little maid,
How many may you be?'
'How many? Seven in all,' she said,
And wondering looked at me.

'And where are they? I pray you tell.'
She answered, 'Seven are we;
And two of us at Conway dwell,
And two are gone to sea.

'Two of us in the church-yard lie,
My sister and my brother;
And, in the church-yard cottage, I
Dwell near them with my mother.'

'You say that two at Conway dwell,
And two are gone to sea,
Yet ye are seven! I pray you tell,
Sweet Maid, how this may be.'

Then did the little Maid reply,
'Seven boys and girls are we;
Two of us in the church-yard lie,
Beneath the church-yard tree.'

'You run about, my little Maid,
Your limbs they are alive;
If two are in the church-yard laid,
Then ye are only five.'

'Their graves are green, they may be seen,'
The little Maid replied,
'Twelve steps or more from my mother's door,
And they are side by side.

'My stockings there I often knit,
My kerchief there I hem;
And there upon the ground I sit,
And sing a song to them.

'And often after sun-set, Sir,
When it is light and fair,
I take my little porringer,
And eat my supper there.

'The first that died was sister Jane;
In bed she moaning lay,
Till God released her of her pain;
And then she went away.

'So in the church-yard she was laid;
And, when the grass was dry,
Together round her grave we played,
My brother John and I.

'And when the ground was white with snow,
And I could run and slide,
My brother John was forced to go,
And he lies by her side.'

'How many are you, then,' said I,
'If they two are in heaven?'
Quick was the little Maid's reply,
'O Master! we are seven.'

'But they are dead; those two are dead!
Their spirits are in heaven!'
'Twas throwing words away; for still
The little Maid would have her will,
And said, 'Nay, we are seven!'

W.B. Yeats
HE WISHES FOR THE CLOTHS OF HEAVEN

Had I the heavens' embroidered cloths,
Enwrought with golden and silver light,
The blue and the dim and the dark cloths
Of night and light and the half-light,
I would spread the cloths under your feet:
But I, being poor, have only my dreams;
I have spread my dreams under your feet;
Tread softly because you tread on my dreams.

ACKNOWLEDGEMENTS

John Murray (Publishers) Ltd for 'How To Get On In Society' from *Collected Poems* by John Betjeman

Century Hutchinson Ltd for 'Hospital For Defectives' from *Selected Poems* by Thomas Blackburn

Martin Secker & Warburg Limited for 'Come Softly To My Wake' by Christy Brown

David Higham Associates Limited for 'Ballad Of The Breadman' from *Collected Poems* by Charles Causley (Macmillan)

Century Hutchinson Ltd for 'Pre-Existence' from *Collected Poems* by Frances Cornford

Associated Book Publishers (UK) Ltd for 'Lie In The Dark And Listen' from *Collected Verse* by Noel Coward (Methuen London)

Abingdon Press for 'The Secret' by R.S. Cushman from *Spiritual Hilltops* (©1932)

Faber & Faber Ltd for 'Journey Of The Magi' from *Collected Poems 1909-62* by T.S. Eliot

Macmillan Publishing Company for 'Gypsies' by Rachel Field from her *Poems* (New York: Macmillan 1957)

Pat Flower for 'Tir Na N-Og' by Robin Flower

Jonathan Cape Ltd and the Estate of Robert Frost for 'Stopping By Woods On A Snowy Evening' from *The Poetry of Robert Frost*, edited by Edward Connery Lathem

A.P. Watt Ltd on behalf of the Executors of the Estate of
Robert Graves for his poem 'Welsh Incident' from his
Collected Poems (1975)

Richard Scott Simon Ltd and the Joyce Grenfell Memorial
Trust 1983 for 'Time' from *Turn Back the Clock*
(Macmillan © Joyce Grenfell Memorial Trust 1983)

Mrs Hodgson and Macmillan, London and Basingstoke, for
'Time, You Old Gypsy Man' from *Collected Poems* by
Ralph Hodgson

Professor Edward Lowbury for his poem 'The Last Day'

Phyllis M. McCormack for her poem 'Look Closer'

Chatto and Windus for 'Lone Dog' from *Songs to Save a Soul*
by Irene McLeod

David Higham Associates Limited for 'Meeting Point' from
Collected Poems by Louis Macneice (Faber & Faber)

The Society of Authors as the literary representative of the
Estate of John Masefield for his poem 'Cargoes'

The Estate of Edna St Vincent Millay for her poem 'Time
Does Not Bring Relief'

The Estate of Alice Duer Miller for her poem 'The White
Cliffs'

Faber & Faber Ltd for 'The Horses' from *The Collected
Poems of Edwin Muir*

John Murray (Publishers) Ltd for 'The Old Grey Squirrel'

from *Collected Poems* by Alfred Noyes

Century Hutchinson Ltd for 'The Rude Potato' by Ruth Pitter

Jonathan Cape Ltd for 'Naming of Parts' from *A Map of Verona* by Henry Reed

Susan Shanks for 'The Other Little Boats' by Edward Shanks

Sidgwick & Jackson Ltd for 'Christmas Legend' by Frank Sidgwick

Associated Book Publishers (UK) Ltd and Jon Silkin for his poem 'Death Of A Son' from his *Poems New and Selected*

The National Poetry Foundation (27 Mill Road, Fareham, Hants PO16 O'TH) for 'Consumer Complaint' by C. Marjorie Smith, from *Turn Any Stone*

John Smith for his poem 'Somewhere Around Christmas' from *A Landscape of My Own* (Robson Books)

Janet Rance and Curtis Brown, London for 'The Cul de Sac' from *The Glass Blower* by Jan Struther

David Higham Associates Limited for 'Do Not Go Gentle Into That Good Night' from *Collected Poems* by Dylan Thomas (J.M. Dent)

Lorna Wood for her poem 'To A Descendant'

A.P. Watt Ltd on behalf of Michael B. Yeats and Macmillan London Ltd for 'He Wishes For The Cloths Of Heaven' from *The Collected Poems of W.B. Yeats*

INDEX OF FIRST LINES AND TITLES

Where there is an asterisk against an entry it indicates that the first line is also the title of the poem